Mandy Steward

THRASHING ABOUT WITH GOD

FINDING FAITH on the OTHER SIDE of everything

David C Cook

transforming lives together

THRASHING ABOUT WITH GOD
Published by David C Cook
4050 Lee Vance View
Colorado Springs, CO 80918 U.S.A.

David C Cook Distribution Canada
55 Woodslee Avenue, Paris, Ontario, Canada N3L 3E5

David C Cook U.K., Kingsway Communications
Eastbourne, East Sussex BN23 6NT, England

The graphic circle C logo is a registered trademark of David C Cook.

The website addresses recommended throughout this book are offered as a
resource to you. These websites are not intended in any way to be or imply an
endorsement on the part of David C Cook, nor do we vouch for their content.

LCCN 2013938615
ISBN 978-0-7814-0825-7
eISBN 978-1-4347-0718-5

© 2013 Mandy Steward
Published in association with the literary agency of WordServe Literary
Group, Ltd., 10152 S. Knoll Circle, Highlands Ranch, CO 80130.

The Team: Don Pape, John Blase, Amy Konyndyk,
Nick Lee, Tonya Osterhouse, Karen Athen
Cover Design: Nick Lee
Cover Photo: Mandy Steward

Printed in the United States of America
First Edition 2013

1 2 3 4 5 6 7 8 9 10

080113

To she who sits in the dark place with me.
To he who gives me space.

Contents

Chapter One

Dear Friend

I really want to write this book for you. I really want to invite you onto a narrow path of your own. I really want to convince you of a grace that allows for far more mess than you and I are even initially comfortable with. To remind you that while we technically cannot move out from under that grace once we've accepted it, sometimes it sure feels as if we have. There is a problem, though, in my periodic bouts of wanting to write for you, and that is that I am often supposing that your faith will play out according to my own. I caught myself doing this just yesterday.

A friend of mine wrote a blog post talking about his struggle to find his identity as an artist. He mentioned all the artistic hats he has tried to wear over the past few years, and he questioned whether any of those were what he should actually be doing with his life. Then he mentioned Jesus and how Jesus didn't die so he could wear an artistic hat; He died so we could be like Him.

I read the post and felt icky inside. I tried to make sense of why I was feeling that way. I could totally relate to being an artist who felt spun around by all the different possible roads to run down. Which to focus on? Who to be? How do I make any of these artistic pursuits "my very own"? But I couldn't relate to the part about Jesus. I disagreed.

I do believe Jesus died so I could be an artist. I do believe God pursued me in this way because He knew it was the only way I would be able to believe in a grace that was big enough to use even me. I do believe that if it weren't for reading Galatians and becoming convinced of His grace for me, I never would have had the guts to write like I am writing now, and I so badly want to write with honesty. I do believe Jesus died so we could feel freed up to go after life to the full, so we would feel equipped to take risks and not beat ourselves up when we fail. He didn't die to make our lives look perfect. He died so we could stop feeling as if our lives have to be perfect for them to mean something.

I felt panic reading my friend's blog post. Is he going to walk away from being an artist? Does he think he needs to search for ways to suffer for Christ instead of live for Him? Is he trying to rid himself of everything he enjoys so he can be sure he's matching Jesus hurt for hurt? Is he trying to perform his way into a life that looks like Christ's and only pursue his art after he achieves this impossible perfection? Cue the feelings of fear and worry and despair. I had to stop him. I had to make sure he wasn't choosing legalism over love. I had to step in front of the train before it took him to a destination I felt sure he didn't want to go to. My intentions were good—a heartfelt plea for a dear friend who might be lost in a jungle he didn't intend to end up in—but there was a piece of me that was feeling a burden not my own.

"He doesn't need you," my friend Teresa reminded me shortly after I left a couple of comments on my friend's blog post and was still feeling uneasy about it all. I wasn't sure which "he" she was referring to. Was the "he" God, or was the "he" my artist friend who wrote the post? I decided it didn't matter. Both of them didn't need me. And you, dear reader of this book, you don't need me either.

I sat for a while in silence thinking about all this. I kind of maniacally laughed, wondering why I write at all then. Why create if I'm not needed? I realized this isn't what Teresa meant. It isn't that the words God (the Muse) gives me can't be used; it's that there is no pressure to have the words be perfect, to have the synapses be sterilely constructed. While it's fine for me to write a heartfelt note to my friend, it isn't necessary for me to think that the richness and fullness of the life he has not yet lived are dependent upon me and my words. I don't have to make sure he "gets it" and stew that perhaps his faith isn't going to play out like mine.

The gut wrenching I felt was due to my belief that I must leave a comment, and it must solve everything. Because the Divine has opened my eyes to how He wants to interact with me, I figured I must be sure to open up everyone else's eyes accordingly, even if I had to pry them open with force and prop them open with toothpicks. I'm giggling at how forcefully I can wield the sword of grace, which isn't meant to be a sword at all. The peace I longed for after reading my friend's post could only be present if I left the comment and then walked away and waited on God's timing of my friend's unfolding, knowing the words could be helpful or could not be, and it didn't matter which was the case.

Last night I read the post one more time. I began to see that it could be taken to mean two very different things, depending on how one defines "be like Christ." I became a bit embarrassed that perhaps we were actually on the same page, and I just read his words to mean something they didn't. I knew for a fact my friend was on a similar journey to mine, trying to declare freedom from legalism, so maybe this was just a necessary stop along the way.

There is a song sung by Joni Mitchell called "Both Sides Now." In it she discusses the very opposite ways we can look at the exact same thing. She talks about love and how she has been able to see it as both something to throw herself into and something to protect herself from. I think it's wise to realize this is true of God's love for me. God has been both someone to throw myself into and to protect myself from. I use her lyrics, superimposing God's name where appropriate:

I've looked at God from both sides now
From up and down, and still somehow
It's God's illusions I recall.
I really don't know God at all.[1]

In any sort of deep contemplation, it's easy to get turned all topsy-turvy. Read philosophy for too long, and you'll begin to wonder if you even exist. I do this with my faith. I think I have something figured out and that I should stand boldly on that truth, and then the tables get turned, and I'm standing on my head and seeing a completely different angle of who the Divine is and what that means to my life.

I realize that this is what happened with me yesterday. I had God figured out. I had grace understood. I read my friend's post and felt 99 percent sure that someone living in grace could not write such a post. I felt it necessary to set him right and make sure he understood what I was saying. I had to know if he was wrong, so I could know if he needed my help.

Oh what a slip-sloppy mess I made. What a bumbling-fumbling way to stir a pot I didn't even need to have my hands in. So I back up. I see that initially I was acting out of love, and I give myself the benefit of the doubt. I laugh at myself lovingly and wrap my arm around my own shoulder and say, "You sure are a passionate young thing, aren't you?"

There is no need to get down off my high horse, for I have already fallen in a little pile of knees and elbows below. So I just dust myself off and thank God I'm not injured, only a bit rattled. I realize our journeys, as humans, are interwoven, but the stories all play out differently, and I don't have the script. I just have my own completed scenes and the completed scenes of others who have gone before me. They give me insight but not formulas.

There is a scene in the book *The Horse and His Boy* from C. S. Lewis's series The Chronicles of Narnia. The boy Shasta is talking to something, but he doesn't quite know what it is. He wonders if it's his imagination, if it's a giant. He can't see the creature in the dark, but he can feel its breath. The thing asks Shasta to tell him why he is so distraught. Shasta relays the whole frightening story. How one bad thing after another has happened, ending with Aravis the horse being wounded by a lion. The voice of the thing ends up sharing with Shasta that it was he who wounded Aravis. The voice was the lion.

"But what for?" Shasta asks.

"Child," the Voice says, "I am telling you your story, not hers. I tell no-one any story but his own."[2]

I think of this giant lion, and I think perhaps he is the voice of the Divine. A voice that is telling me, "Mandy, I'm not telling you why your friend who wrote the blog post needed to let go of the artistic hats and focus on being like Jesus. But for some reason that thought resonated with him, and he felt closer to Me because of it, and that's okay."

The voice of the Divine inside me continues, "There's a lot about other people's stories I'm not telling you. I'm not telling you why so many Jewish people were tortured in concentration camps; why Jay-Z grew up on the streets, hustling drugs to help feed and clothe his family; or why Virginia Woolf and Sylvia Plath committed suicide. What I am telling you is *your* story, and your story happens to involve a girl who has a season of life when she skips out on church, leaves her small group, closes up her Bible, and gets really messy with her faith. You don't have to stress that everyone else's story may not look like yours. You don't have to try to force them to step into your precise footprint impressions on the narrow road you walk. I don't need you to understand why someone else's story may involve the exact opposite actions: going to church, joining a small group, opening their Bible, and cleaning up their messy life. I just need you to live out your own story."

A couple of days ago, my kids and I took a walk to get donuts for breakfast with some money that my mom had sent them. The three oldest insisted on riding scooters, because "It's more fun that way!" After we got our box of donuts, we walked a block or so to a tiny little park with concrete benches. We sat there in the shade and snacked on our donuts. When we finished, I asked Charis if she would be willing to throw our trash away in the Dumpster. She said she didn't want to because she was scared that flies might fly out when she opened the lid. So I turned to her older sister, Zoe, and asked if she'd be willing to throw the trash away. She held out her hand to take it and then asked, "Where is the trash can?"

I pointed to the Dumpster, which was to my right. She looked at it and then took off as fast as she could down the sidewalk toward the left. In my impatience, I made an assumption that she was directly disobeying me. I hollered out, "Forget it, Zoe. Never mind." Then I turned to Nehemiah and said, "Would you be willing to throw the trash away?"

He was elated. "Sure! I'll do it."

I told Zoe to hand over the trash to Nehemiah, and she was furious. "You told me I could do it. Why won't you let me do it?"

"Because, Zoe, I told you the Dumpster was one way, and then you took off in the opposite direction. I assumed you weren't listening, so I decided to give 'Miah a chance at it."

She was livid. She threw down her scooter and stomped the trash over to Nehemiah. "You didn't even give me a chance. I wanted to ride on the smooth parking lot, so I was just going to ride to the end of the sidewalk and then zoom across the parking lot. I was going a different way at first, but I was still going to end up where you wanted me."

I think I do this with other people, but with Christians in particular. I look at them and think, *If you're veering off to the left, there is no way you are ever going to make it to the narrow gate that is over my right shoulder. I specifically know you can't be going that way, because God told me we must go this way. You're way off track.* I'm so busy looking for a certain path to be followed that I don't realize there are multiple ways of getting to the same exact place. And God is telling me, "It's not your story. They don't need you to reroute their stories to match yours."

I really want there to be a formulaic way to calculate things like grace and God's voice and timing. I really want to be able to say to you, "Why, my dear friend, all you need to know is that $X + Y$ always equals Z," but I can't, because yesterday when I did the math, $X + Y$ equaled N, and I have no idea why. Just yesterday that equation looked like something I had mastered, but it seems my formulas are just illusions of how God operates, so most times I'm just making best guesses.

I warn you, this book in your hands contains no magical power except for the magical power you bring to it. This book you hold in your hands is a reminder that your story remains unfinished, and you have the capacity to write it precisely how you've been longing to write it. This book cannot give you answers, but it can reintroduce you to a Divine indwelling that burns with the chance to be known, explored, battled, embraced, questioned, pursued, and loved. You don't need my formulas. You don't need the Mandy Steward approach. You don't need another set of rules and regulations, of laws and decrees. You need to explore a messy grace that knows no limits. That says, "Yes, even in the valley of the shadow of death, I am still holding on, because I know what I want, and I'm relentless in going after it. Who will listen to me, if not me? I've tried a lot of different ways, but now I'm ready to try my own way."

As Ralph Waldo Emerson said so well in his poem, "Gnothi Seauton," "Give up to thy soul / Let it have its way— / It is, I tell theo, God himself."

Chapter Two

Full

I distinctly remember the "Beware of God" girl in high school. She occasionally wore a black shirt with strong white lettering. The letters spelled "Beware of God" across her tiny chest. It was a bold statement, and one that certainly got my attention. In fact, I think I kind of followed her around like a lost puppy, only if you had asked me at the time, I thought she was the one who was lost and searching for someone to follow. She was younger than I was, my upperclassman trumping her freshman status. Her hair was bleached blonde, dark roots betraying her fake yellows. Her eyes were always heavily outlined in black eyeliner, which I assumed was a sign of rebellion and angst. She seemed a bit hollow, as if something had been carved out from behind her eyes where life was supposed to dance.

I felt drawn to her, her magnetic powers scooting me across slick high school hallways and pulling me in close. If I had to guess, I would say her name was Amanda, but I can't be sure. I don't believe we ever officially met. I always saw her in the same place, sitting on the waist-high walls that partitioned off the cafeteria from the rest of the school. Sitting on the waist-high walls that no one was supposed to sit on. She was a rule breaker.

Her shirt spoke to me, and with that shirt, she became the epitome of the "unsaved" person we learned so much about in Sunday school and church youth group. She represented the quintessential non-Christian to me at the time, even though, looking back now, I have no clue if my assumptions were true. What I do know is that her shirt stirred up emotions in me that I didn't want around. I thought she needed saving, and I thought I was just the right person to do so. What I was really battling was opposition to my beliefs and the frantic desire within me to prove I was, in fact, right.

She haunted me a little, this girl, her "Beware of God" shining like headlights, superimposing its capitalized statement over all the Christian answers I had memorized. She made me want to live my faith out a little louder, because if I could be a little louder, maybe I could be a little surer.

One day I stood in front of slamming lockers at the end of a school day and told passing students that God loved them, to which one guy spouted back at me, "Go to hell!" I wore this "persecution" like a badge of honor and soaked up the sympathy of my Christian cohorts, who wrapped arms around my shoulders and said, "Of course he was out of line to say that," and "Of course he clearly needs God's love more than anything."

I shook my head in confusion at one certain churchgoing friend of mine who said, "Maybe you need to back off a bit." Me? No way! *He* should be apologizing to *me*.

I think about the younger me, and my tendency is to be a bit embarrassed by her overenergetic enthusiasm. She seems cheerleaderish now, shaking black-and-white pom-poms in the faces of those whose lives were lived in the gray areas. I shook plastic pom-poms of polished love and shiny answers in unsuspecting faces and then wondered why they looked a bit turned off. This is the same Mandy who kept a stack of Christian tracts and pass-it-on Scripture cards in a special place on her bookshelf at home. Oh, believe me, she was primed to get the Word out.

But here is what I love about her: I love that she got disrupted and disturbed by the lives of those around her. I love that "Beware of God" girl broke something inside her. I love that "Go to hell!" boy's words stung her. For though she wasn't brave enough to voice questions out loud, and though she was still too timid to admit there were unaddressed issues within, she was beginning the search for a faith and a God she could stomach in the face of life's creeping darkness. She was not blind to the darkness.

Nearly fifteen years later, I feel as if I'm the one slipping the tight black T-shirt over my head and squeezing my arms through freshman-sized armholes. The bottom black hem barely covers my belly button, and the white letters feel so hot I imagine they are being branded into my chest. I hoist myself up onto the cafeteria wall, and I pull out a pocket mirror and apply thick eyeliner. I am climbing into the brunt of what haunted me about that T-shirt, and I'm not backing down until I get some clarity, until I get some peace.

Because here's the crux of it all: my God hasn't proved to be safe, and my Christian answers haven't proved to be enough. There have been times when doing the "right" thing and "playing by the rules" most certainly did not land me in the place of a thriving and vibrant life to the full. I have stayed off cafeteria walls my whole life, only to find that maybe that streaked-blonde freshman could have given me some sanity if I had just had the guts to see my own lostness in hers.

The playing field has been leveled, and I don't want the answers I'm supposed to have. I want the ones that actually work. Or perhaps I want to know that there actually are no blanket, black-and-white answers for cleaning up the messiness I face. Namely, I want to breathe again. As Anne Lamott says, "There is a lot to be said for desperation.... The main gift is a willingness to give up the conviction that you are right, and that God thinks so, too, and hates the people who are driving you crazy."[1]

I am desperate.

And maybe you are too.

Maybe you've been secretly stalking your own "Beware of God" girl, wishing you had the boldness to speak the truth that haunts you down deep. Maybe you've been secretly jealous of those "Go to hell!" boys who get to say what they think without wondering if they themselves will go to hell for doing so. Maybe you've been secretly whispering questions but covering them up with answers you've been told will work if you just believe hard enough.

And you're tired.

You're tired of pretending.

You're tired of building walls around your heart.

You're tired of spitting out right answers for others when your own well has gone dry. Bone dry.

You're tired of thinking the dreams you long to step into aren't holy enough to warrant action.

You're tired of doing the Christian thing. You're tired of religiously giving and sacrificing and having nothing left to feed yourself.

But you're also terrified. Terrified that coming clean means admitting you have a selfish, sinful ego like everyone else. You're sure that your buried truths negate your appreciation for a Savior who died for you. Said Savior who was *supposed* to set you free. And you whisper, really quietly, so that God Himself, should He happen to be in the neighborhood, can't hear you: "Where's my freedom? Where's my life to the full? Where am *I* in all this living?"

I want you to know what you are doing right now is brave. Really and truly brave. And I want to invite you up onto cafeteria walls with me. I have an extra T-shirt, and if we sit up here together, they'll have a much harder time getting us to come down. Sometimes you have to rage against the machine before you can make your peace with it, and you've been quiet and scared and polite for a really long time. I just want you to know there ain't nothing wrong with a little bit of soul-searching.

We get up here, together, on this wall, and we realize we're high enough to drown out all the other voices. The *shoulds*, the *have-tos*, the *musts* that others shout at us. We can't hear them up here. We get on to the brave business of digging into our own hearts' questions. Of asking God, "Why is there so much to be afraid of? Why aren't You safer? What if I'd rather not believe You exist at all?" Of listening to the fears and furies that have been waging war on our insides in a battle to be heard. We give questions voice, and we find that when we do, when we step into the darker, unexplored sides of God, the mystery doesn't swallow us as we dreamed it might, but it opens up a whole new world of wooing adventures.

So let them think our eyes are hollow for a bit, because, friend, we've got some dancing to do down deep. You are not alone. We go in together. We come out together. Changed.

When I was a freshman and sophomore in college, I took a required two-year course called Humanities. The purpose of the course was to look back on the history of humanity and study how people have answered the following questions:

- What does it mean to be fully human?
- Is there a God, who is God, and can a person know God?
- What responsibilities do we, as both part of creation and stewards of it, have to the rest of the created order?
- How does one relate to one's fellow human beings?
- How does one answer life's inescapable questions— of love, hate, belonging, vocation, meaning, death?

I return to these key questions often as I'm going about my normal, everyday life. The questions haunt me because they suggest there is something much more epic going on than what seems to occur in the confines of paying taxes, attending church, and doing the dishes.

There is more, right? Please, someone tell me there is more. And yet, if there is more to this life, maybe I don't want to know about it, because I feel pretty trapped by the ordinary. I don't want to know there is more if I don't have access to it.

There is a phrase that sums up "the more" for me. It's a phrase that has resurfaced time and again during my thirty-two years of life. It comes from the Bible, but it's a phrase I'm confident any human can relate to. It is simply "life to the full." In context, it is Jesus talking, and the full verse reads, "The thief comes only to steal and kill and destroy; I have come that they may have life, and have it to the full" (John 10:10).

It is what we want, isn't it? It's why we're up here on this rebel wall in our black T-shirts. Maybe it's why Jacob wrestled with God. We're hard-pressed to nail down exactly what "life to the full" looks like, but we know we want it. We're holding out for our blessing.

It labors my breathing sometimes, I want it so badly, especially on the days where all I seem to have to work with are the mediums of dirty laundry, bills that need paid, necessary home repairs, and relational dissatisfaction and disapproval. There is dust falling faster than I can ever clean it, and I'm smothering under a layer of "this is just how things will have to be, so deal with it."

It reminds me of the conversation that occurs with my four kids when it's time to clean up all that we have played with in a day. There are times when I do a really poor job of easing them into this process. I get overwhelmed by the number of piles of toys that have been dragged out and then abandoned. Five decks of playing cards are strewn through living room, kitchen, stairwell, bathroom, hallways, and bedrooms. How did this Queen of Hearts make it into the bathroom sink? Books are spread over couch tops, while doodled pieces of paper and broken crayons, Matchbox car pileups, LEGOs, blocks, and abandoned socks and shoes are halfway swallowed up by dark couch underbellies. I survey the premises and hear the words fly out of my mouth that my dad used to say to me when I had my own messy room to deal with: "It looks like a tornado came through here. We need to stop everything we're doing and clean this up."

It's usually my youngest daughter and my oldest son (my middle kids) who have the hardest time with it. And as they spiral into their reactions, I realize instantly that this is how I inwardly react when life doesn't pan out as I had hoped. Folded arms, dropped head, stomping feet. My son huffs and puffs his way up the stairs. "I hate cleaning up," he yells.

My daughter is more verbal. She tells me how it is. Her voice gets faster and louder with every sentence. "Just when we were starting to play something really fun, you make us stop and clean up. I hate it when you do this. And look, would you just look at all we have to clean? There are toys everywhere!"

Perhaps this isn't the best time for me to tell her that *she* is the one who got them all out, but I tell her anyway, amused that she thinks this is so unfair. I tell her that it's not my fault they never put anything away when they are done with it. One day I will learn to hold my tongue, but not today.

I'm sorry to say I enrage her. "Fine, then," she says. "Just throw all our toys away. I don't want them. I don't ever want to play with them again. I hate toys! People just make them to ruin little kids' lives. I wish they didn't even make toys. I hate my life. I wish I was dead."

Now this has gotten completely out of hand. I want to tell her she's not allowed to say that. I want to tell her I hate it when she says things like that about herself. I want to tell her they're just toys.

Instead, I watch as she squeezes her little fists tight against her side, and her face turns red with fury. I realize to her they are not *just* toys. I realize to her they constitute an insurmountable task. I realize to her they were fun moment after fun moment after fun moment, and they're now returning to bite her in the butt. I realize to her this mess is the unexpected change of plans, the surprise inconvenience, the crumbling of her perfect little imagination world.

I watch and I realize this is largely how I feel about my own life sometimes.

On these days, I want to stomp my own feet, clench my own fists, scream my own red-faced scream, "Jesus, You, Sir, are a liar. Where is my life to the full You promised?"

This is quickly followed by a Christian cloud of guilt. How could I even dare to include *Jesus* and *liar* in the same sentence, let alone curse His great cosmic plan for humanity?

For years this is where it would end. It would end in guilt. And the guilt would send me running back to the comfortable, albeit empty and boring, life I knew so well. If I could only understand God more, if I could only obey Him more, if I could only serve and sacrifice more, if I could only accept my lot in life, stay off cafeteria walls, and learn to be content. If I could only just play nice and clean up my Matchbox cars when I'm done with them, then perhaps I could nail down this ever-elusive life to the full.

I've thought a lot about when it was that I noticed I was empty, and I honestly can't pinpoint an exact moment. Maybe it was my final semester of college and my first day of class, when one of my professors, John Eldredge, played U2's "I Still Haven't Found What I'm Looking For," and the lyrics made me cry in complete surrender to the fact that I was twenty-one and still had no answers to show for it.

Maybe it was when my family arrived in Southern California, beaten down from a risky cross-country move that ended in our entire U-Haul truck being stolen. Maybe it was in the weeks to follow, when sickness and injury and heartache and unmet promises would bombard us, and my anger toward God would burn.

Maybe it was at the birth of my fourth child, and in the depression and anger that would follow as I realized I could no longer keep all the plates spinning.

Maybe it was in the shadows of embarrassment as I witnessed the broken plates all around me, and the only solution I knew was the one I had used so often in my life—to act as if nothing had happened and to find more plates to spin.

Maybe it was when I realized that that solution was no longer good enough.

It was a culmination of all these events that alerted me to the fact that I was plummeting into a life of disappointment, destruction, and status-quo survival. I'm grateful that the phrase "life to the full" never left me. I would hear it at the oddest of times. I would weep for it, curse at it, stare dumbfounded toward it, but for some reason, I never gave up on it. It never gave up on me. And then at some point, it was as if I awakened to it. It felt closer than ever before. I felt rightful ownership toward it.

Jesus and His promises of a full life really disappointed some people. The Jews wanted a king who would rule politically and save them culturally, and Jesus appeared to be so little like this royalty they longed for. But He always said that if people could just have "eyes to see" and "ears to hear," they could see God's kingdom *now*, on earth.

I'm thinking about Jesus and His famous Sermon on the Mount. I'm thinking specifically about the narrow and wide gates He spoke of in Matthew 7:13–14. Those verses have a history of sounding so condemning to me: "Enter through the narrow gate. For wide is the gate and broad is the road that leads to destruction, and many enter through it. But small is the gate and narrow the road that leads to life, and only a few find it."

I'm hearing it differently today, though, as if with new ears. I'm wondering if maybe this narrow gate leads to that full life we're longing for and chasing after. I'm wondering if the entrance is just on the other side of these scaled cafeteria walls. I'm wondering if the reason the wide gate is so wide is because it's far easier to take things at face value. To see strewn toys. To see hard-earned savings drained by having to buy new car tires. To see tornadoes rip apart homes. To see betrayal in relationships. To see sickness and depression. The wide-gate dwellers believe that when these things happen, it's because they are doing something wrong. If they can just live the "right" way and clean things up a bit, then everything will eventually fall into place. "Just try harder" is their motto.

"Paige," I said over the phone to a college friend I had recently reconnected with after eight years, "it's like there have always been two teams, God and humanity, and I've felt thus far that I am obligated to play on God's team. I have to uphold His rules, His values, His answers. I have to pretend as though that's all working for me. I

29

haven't allowed myself the honest glance at this very human part of me that has hurts and hang-ups and desires and dreams, because to do so would be betraying God's team.

"And now, well, now it's like I've finally admitted and surrendered to my humanity. And I just want to pull us all into one big hug and say, 'Man, we're a crazy, sordid, thrashing-about bunch, aren't we? How desperate we are to survive, to thrive, to make a name for ourselves. To have a life that is valued, a life that matters. How much we all really do have in common.'

"And the crazy thing, Paige, is that I don't feel like God's mad at me for changing teams. I don't feel like He's ashamed or that He feels betrayed at all. I feel like He's right here with me, and the illusion of teams was just that, an illusion. Some days I really feel the fluidity of us all being one with God. Like He gets us. Like He's okay that I'm human. Like He really wants to meet me there and fill me there, in the midst of all my mess. That if Jesus means anything, He means God's not distant from humanity. He's made His way to us. He's 'one of us,' just like Joan Osborne suggests."[2]

I have lived the empty life of pretending and feeling like I must be sitting the bench on God's team because I'm just not praying enough or reading my Bible enough or sacrificing enough to get access to the good life He speaks of. I have lived this way, but I don't want to anymore.

I figure if the card I've been played is the bent, good-for-nothing Queen of Hearts in the bathroom sink, then maybe I just better figure out how to make something of it. Figure out how to have eyes to see it for treasure. Figure out how to get to walking toward that narrow gate.

Maybe, just maybe, a full life doesn't necessitate a perfect life. Maybe we don't have to do it the "right" way. Maybe we can learn to have ears to hear the hurt, the pain, the questions, the fear, the unfairness of adventures that require our ever-unfolding bravery, a bravery that introduces us to hidden-kingdom fulfillment. The kingdom where fairy tales are birthed, like Cinderellas masked in rags or fierce swans mistaken for ugly ducklings.

I don't think the "full" in "life to the full" is ever fulfilled. It's like my friend Susie says: "I find I'm constantly searching, but not sure what for." I haven't yet satisfied my thirst. Instead, it's a mysterious spring I drink from regularly, returning as needed.

Consider this book a note passed to you during class when the teacher wasn't looking. A note beckoning you to cafeteria walls and narrow-gate portals. A note of permission to live out your own unique version of life to the full. In summary, the note reads,

Dear Friend,

Maybe you've lost your shoes and socks in the darkness of couch underbellies, and you've been lectured by angry, misunderstanding moms to tow the line and pull your shoes back out and clean up this mess of a life. But you know you are doing your best. So you slap your barefooted best efforts, one foot at a time, on that dirty road that leads to the narrow gate, even if it strays from the path you've been told is right, and you become determined to join or create a community of those who speak your language, who aren't afraid to search for truth no matter how dark and mysterious it gets. May you have courage to do what's in your heart. May you have eyes to see a miracle, a gift, a secret message when it comes, and may you have ears to hear the words, "You are loved, and you are never alone."

Yours Truly,
A Fellow "Beware of God" Girl

Chapter Three

You

"I just don't feel like going to church anymore. I don't know if I can sit through another service. Maybe I should sign up to work in the nursery instead."

"Ah, yes, because that would really be a good time for you." His voice dripped with sarcasm. "Maybe you should just work out your frustration in service and dedication. That sounds like a great idea."

My husband knows me well. I had to laugh at myself. Did I really think the answer my heart was looking for was one more accomplishment performed for God? I envisioned myself standing up, the back of my head and the back of my heels pressed firmly against a white wall, while God stands with a pencil, etching a dark line directly at the crown of my head. He pats me on the head in a detached, cheeky sort of manner and says, "Well done, good and faithful servant. You have rocked the babies to make up for your lame attempt to skip out on my church services." And then He writes "Mandy Steward, Nursery Worker" beside the pencil line and dates it. He even puts a little star beside it so we can both remember the day I gave it my all for the glory of God.

Certainly this doesn't mean that every woman or man who has ever rocked babies in a church nursery was doing it out of dead faith, empty devotion, or legalistic extremes, but for me, this would have been the case. Perhaps you can recall a time you resorted to empty actions in an attempt to please God and grasp at some sort of happiness and meaning for your life. "It's not about me or about what I want," we tell ourselves. "It's all about God."

But I believe in me. This you must know. I believe in the me who is battered and bruised and imprisoned from years of thinking it was sinful to believe in me. My pastor for two years of my life was a man by the name of Rick Warren. I loved my time learning from him. It was a pivotal time in my life, a time when ten years of growth were shoved into a mere two. Rick Warren wrote a book called *The Purpose Driven Life,* and it begins with these words: "It's not about you."[1] Those words came back to me today as I was sitting and journaling. Only they came to me in a very shocking, twisted sort of way. They came to me like this: "It *is* about you. Right now, you need to make it about you."

I would be lying if I told you I don't feel like a dirty traitor for going against a book that has sold millions of copies and has been translated into several different languages and has had life-changing impact on countless others. I would be lying if I told you I don't feel sheepish for counteroffering my own words for the words of a pastor I do so respect. But I also can't deny the feeling of relief that washed over me as I sat on my well-stained brown leather couch with ripped seams, my feet tucked into soft black slippers, my journal cradled on my lap, and my pen putting words onto paper faster than I can be held responsible for.

The main reason that life has started taking on any semblance of fullness for me is because I have made it about me. I will make no apology for those words today. Come back tomorrow. I might think otherwise. But today ... today I know that this is the truth. I haven't set out selfishly like a bratty child, claiming my toys as mine and mine alone, snatching them from the hands of other, unsuspecting toddlers. I haven't plundered, killed, or tortured to stake my territory. I have merely chosen to listen to my heart for the first time in a long time.

I recently shared a quote over Twitter from the great philosopher Napoleon Dynamite: "Follow your heart, Pedro. That's what I do."[2] I was met instantly with a reply from a man who quoted for me a scripture from the Bible that said, "The heart is deceitful above all things" (Jer. 17:9). His response spoke volumes to me. *Yes, this is appropriate,* I thought. It is a real-life example of the answer I have given myself for years.

Don't trust yourself. Don't listen to yourself. Seek answers outside of yourself. Let others who are wiser and older and likely male feed you answers. Read the Bible the way these others read the Bible. Let them tell you what it says. You aren't able to comprehend it on your own. You aren't able to interpret such holy words. You cannot be trusted. Your desires, your hopes, your blowing-out-the-candles birthday wishes—they are silly and foolish and childish. They are fantasy in a world of reality. They are frivolity in a world that is serious business. You don't matter. God matters. It's not about you.

I wrote a blog post recently about my experiences with yoga as a Christian. At one point I mentioned that yoga really is more about being in touch with yourself and working through your own issues than it is about who you're praying to or what set of beliefs you adhere to or what poses you are capable of or how strong or flexible you are or how long you can meditate. It's about listening to yourself. You honor your limitations, and you ignore your ego. A woman responded to my post in the comments saying, "Faith isn't about us or being 'in touch with yourself.' Christian faith is about the gospel.

"So, I guess my question(s) to you is/are: How do you see the gospel being played out and/or actually transforming your life through yoga? Why even dance around something so dangerous? Why not set apart that time just for prayer and digging into the Word and exercise another way?"

I responded to her several days later. It took me a while to really consider her questions.

"Yes, faith may be about the gospel, about redemption, but if I lose touch with myself and where I'm at in the midst of upholding the gospel, then the gospel isn't actually good news for me at all. It's just something I've memorized. When the gospel meets me where I'm really at, with my doubts and my mistakes and my hang-ups, that's when it's powerful."

I think about a Frederick Buechner quote from his book *Telling the Truth*: "Speaking … not just what we ought to say about the Gospel, not just what it would appear to be in the interests of the Gospel for us to say, but what we have ourselves felt about it."[3]

The truth for me right now is that traditional prayer and "digging into the Word" aren't doing it for me. I know as a Christian I am supposed to uphold those columns of our faith, but I'm finding God has grace for me when I can't. That's good news for me, because I'd hate to lose touch with God.

I wonder if there are others who believe as I have believed. I have family members and friends who are working jobs they don't want to be working, who are living lives they don't want to be living, who have made great sacrifices, but at the cost of what—their very hearts? And this is applauded and worn as a badge of honor. This is our self-prescripted suffering that we, as Christians, must endure, because we are putting God first. Burned-out mothers have more children. Beaten-down fathers continue working desk jobs and being yes-men to bosses they don't respect. Women have busy feet, looking for one more cause to champion tirelessly. Men and women sit in more meetings, make more connections, and wait somewhat patiently for their "big break" to come.

My husband always says to our musician friends, "Move to Nashville. Go be where the songwriters are. Immerse yourself in that culture. Take a risk. Don't sit and wait to get noticed. Go get noticed."

I read a quote recently by Tenneva Jordan that said, "A mother is a person who, seeing there are only four pieces of pie for five people, promptly announces she never did care for pie." I read that quote, and my creative juices start flowing. I think, *I'm not all that great at math, but certainly we could come up with a creative way to divide the pie so we could all have a bit. Especially if it's my grandma's pumpkin pie with a dollop of whipped cream on top.*

This thought, of course, is trailed by that little prick of guilt I've become so familiar with, because what if I'm not the sort of mom who wants to sacrifice everything for my children? What if I'm just not that noble? Do I have to eat my pie hiding in the shadows of a dark closet between coat sleeves and the vacuum cleaner?

I can make anything into a faith challenge. I've become a bit too good at denying myself what I think I want in order to prove to myself I can survive without it. I can easily twist this into my sordid proof that I am living a life that God would approve of.

We do go through dead motions like this sometimes, don't we? We hold on to dead relationships, dead churches, dead actions, dead hearts, and dead-end lives, because if we just have a little more faith in something other than ourselves, then maybe things will change for the better. We fake it until we make it. We kid ourselves that this is what it looks like to have a relationship with God. Look at us. We're a superstitious ball of jokes, holding our breath, crossing our fingers, throwing salt over our shoulders, and not stepping on cracks. Some of us have made a living out of rule making, all because our hearts are supposedly faulty, all because we can't be trusted, all because, despite all costs, our lives cannot be about us. We Eeyore our way through. Thanks, God, for "noticing me."

Is it any wonder we have lost our lives to the full? Life to the full comes about because God loves us so much, He makes it about us. Is it too much to consider that someone might actually want to love on you?

I think about sex. Sex, in its purest form, is not for God. It's a gift from God for us, for humanity, for two souls intertwining in pleasure. When we engage in it purely, we can't help but be brought back to a state of gratitude. It's a breath of fresh air we've been longing to take.

And so it is with the rest of His creation. Things made for our enjoyment, to dazzle our eyes, to please our fingertips, to move our hearts, to entice our ears, to tantalize our taste buds, to make our souls sigh with one waft of a pleasing aroma. It's as if God flirts with us through His creations, asking us to taste and see that He is, in fact, good.

He handcrafted us with wants and desires and gifts and talents in His own creative image, and then He gave us a free will. Choice. Free rein to create the life we innately desire. Wouldn't the greatest sign of appreciation be to take it and make something of it? Something glorious and wonderful? Maybe even to take some risks in going after our hearts' true desires?

I've been going about it all backward. Or maybe I've just interpreted that phrase all wrong. I've been saying, "It's all about God," so I've tried to live a religious life I think He would approve of. I've tried to be holy. I've tried to live out God in my own image, according to the rules. I've taken on more than I needed to in order to please Him. I've suffered and sacrificed in ways that were unnecessary in order to gain His approval or the approval of people. I've made grave, monumental assumptions about what He wants from me in light of how Scripture has been interpreted to me, and I've come up empty and angry and guilt-ridden and bitter. What has my faith gotten me?

I've done it all right and created my own personal penances for the times I've failed, but You haven't held up to Your end of the bargain, God. My life is not full! I'm rubbing the lamp as fast as I can, but no magical genie is emerging. What a hoax.

Last year I wrote a check. A big check. A check that we didn't have the money for. I wrote it in faith. I wrote the check because nearly three years prior to that, I had written a similar check for an even more extensive amount of money, and I had seen God come through. I had seen God, almost overnight, erase an $11,000 debt in our life. At least I attributed it to God, because every good and perfect gift comes from Him, right? It was breathtaking. And I was banking on that same sort of fortune to hit me again, so we could pay off our only remaining credit card.

So I wrote the check, and I set it on my dresser, and I looked at it every day, and I thought, *I wonder how You're going to get us this money, God.* And sometimes, on my less faith-filled days, I would tilt my head and squint a bit intimidatingly at Him like a mafia boss and say in a deep, throaty voice, "You *are* going to get us this money, right?" I was rubbing my lamp and playing my own little game I had gotten so good at. I sincerely hoped this was in God's will for my life. The mafia boss believed it would be in God's best interest.

I raised my internal eyebrows whenever my husband, Tony, would make purchases I didn't deem worthy, because, of course, I was dutifully carrying out my own expenditures with wisdom and restraint. I loathed going to the grocery store, feeling guilty for everything I put in the cart that might not be necessary for our survival. I sat around feeling a bit anxious and tried to dream up get-rich schemes that might help God along in the process.

I read get-rich type books and asked my more wealthy Christian friends and family if they thought it was sinful to desire wealth. I wanted money, and I wanted it as soon as possible. Oh, and I wanted it because, in a small way, I suppose, I had earned it. Hadn't God seen how good I was at denying myself? Hadn't God seen the faithful way we tithed, even over the required 10 percent at times?

One day I found that check I had written. It had slipped underneath the bed with a plastic Batman and a long-forgotten flip-flop. I realized, with a deep sigh of disappointment, that the predated numbers on the check had come and gone. We were past the day on which I had hoped God would provide us with the money. It appeared as if we were going to have to solve this debt problem the hard way—with time and patience and a good old-fashioned thing called a budget. And here I was hoping it was enough to just follow the good-stewardship rules and step out in a strong charismatic faith. Wasn't I following the proper formula, doing just exactly what I'd done three years prior?

It's a difficult life, this bartering with God. He has the pencil tucked behind His ear, the little pink eraser sticking out next to His bushy, white eyebrows. Sometimes I think He's really going for the pencil. I assume my position up against the wall, head raised high. He raises His arm up to His face as if He's reaching for the pencil, but then it turns out He's just yawning, covering His open mouth politely before dropping His arm to His side again. He really had me going that time. I insecurely wonder if His yawning has anything to do with the boring life I'm living.

So I redouble my efforts. I smile at the clerk at the grocery store. I give a five-dollar bill to the man with the cardboard sign standing in the median. I sign up for a Bible-reading plan, because it has been a while since I've read His Book consistently, and don't all authors like to know you've been reading their book? And maybe, just for good measure, I stop buying iTunes songs, because He'd probably want me to use that money for a good cause rather than having a dance party in my living room.

I pull each and every string I can think of, wondering which one is connected to God's arm, so I can get Him to grab that pencil and mark my star on the wall once again. Not once does it occur to me that He may like to hear what I have to say. That He may be interested in my ideas. That He may be waiting on me to cue up the music to my own dance party. That He may be lying on the ground under my bed, squeezed in between the long-forgotten flip-flop and the plastic Batman, wondering if I'll see Him when I pick up the check.

Just for the record, if He was there, I didn't see Him. I missed Him completely.

I imagine Him laughing. Tickled at how often I brush by Him but never even see Him. I'm not sure I want Him anyway. I think I'd rather just have His pencil.

Have I really traded my unique soul in exchange for a pencil to etch the wall?

Do I really want my marks on the wall to be the extent of my life?

Do I really want the cookie-cutter approach? Do I really believe that if Jesus is *the* way, then our roads to get to Him must all look exactly the same? Our lives must all contain the same elements? There must be God's one way to live a good life, and the details must all play out the same? If I do *this*, then God rewards me, and if He doesn't reward me, then I haven't performed to His liking? Is this my life to the full? Penciled-in stars?

What's inside me either matters or it doesn't. Either it is worth listening to or it isn't. Either it is worth exploring or it is worth ignoring. But the decision I make about myself and my worth is a decision that will affect my entire life. If my story doesn't matter internally, my story won't matter to anyone else.

Maybe He *is* handing us that pencil after all, and we're too busy scraping marks on a wall to realize we could be writing a breathtaking novel. We could be writing the story we long to step into.

If we don't write it the way we desire it deep down inside, you can bet it's not going to cosmically emerge into a miraculous unfolding. If you're giving all of yourself away and waiting on God to move the pencil, you may be left as I was: angry, empty, bitter. A compliant Christian with a life lacking fullness.

I won't live like this anymore. You don't have to either.

Chapter Four

Naked

She is small. Compared to the world, compared to the church, compared to institutions, compared to God. And she appears fragile. She steps out of the hot shower and sucks in air as the cold bathroom chills the drops of water on her skin. She rubs her hand on the mirror in one spot, removing the steam that has gathered there. In one small part of the mirror, she now becomes visible. She stands there, naked, and makes herself look, because that's what her college professor told her she should do all those years ago: "I recommend looking at yourself naked in the mirror each morning. A good hard look. A look that chooses to take it all in, even the parts you've been ignoring because you don't want to see. Those parts are you as well."

So she stares. The foggy glass fills back in over her face and she feels smothered. She uses a towel to wipe away all of the fog. She takes a deep breath and meets herself eye to eye. Her skin seems to hang on her body; her eyes look scared. She realizes it isn't necessary that she put herself through this.

She looks closer. She sees the glimmer of white sprouting up among the black forest of her hair. *I'm not old enough to have gray hair,* she thinks. She isn't old enough for a lot of things, it feels like. Isn't she just a kid still? Lost in thought, she raises her hand to her head and begins isolating the glimmering hairs so she can rip them out. One, two, three. She gets bored with the task. There are too many. She makes a mental note to purchase hair dye yet again.

Her eyes pan back from her head to include her whole body. Her head goes blurry as she observes the muscles in her arms and her belly and her legs. They are noticeable. They have never been noticeable. She wonders when they arrived.

She pushes her shoulders back. She is frustrated that they seem more at ease in their hunched state than in their proper elegant position. She realizes that her shoulders pull back her chest, and her chest has always been something to hide. A source of jokes in high school. A source of jokes in her own head now that pregnancies and age have left her body unsure what shape it is to fit in. She curses the college professor. She curses the mirror. She curses the fog she has wiped away. Oh, why did she wipe it away?

But her eyes cannot be peeled away now. She is enamored by a woman she has lost contact with, a woman who has changed so much, she hardly even recognizes her. A woman who has opinions now and a voice and a reason to get out of bed, more so than the reasons that everyone else had provided for her. She turns to the side and reminds her shoulders to stay back out of her ears. She takes a deep breath and lets it out slowly. *This is who you will be traveling with from here on out. Get used to her. Love her. Find the beauty in her. See past her flaws. You must not let her stay trapped in a mere shell. There is more to let free. There is always more.*

Her toes curl beneath her, gripping the floor. The skin on her legs looks pale and splotchy in color. She remembers the scratchy way her fingers felt when she rubbed the cheek of her toddler to say, *I love you.* She felt as if she might hurt him merely by her touch. She felt raw and scratchy. She felt as if she wasn't capable of gliding smoothly through life like she desired. Scratchy, dry winter skin and itchy wool sweaters. The combination was almost too much. Who invented such an unfair combination? She curses the inventor.

She knows what she is really cursing, though. It isn't her professor or the mirror or the dry skin or the wool sweaters. It isn't even the boys who teased her mercilessly in high school, trying to hide the personal attacks under the protection of what sometimes sounded like compliments. It is the unfamiliarity of her own nakedness. The very act of taking time in the transition from wet body to warm, protective clothes. It is the desire to see what truly exists, and yet the uncontainable urge to place her hands over her eyes, spreading fingers just millimeters apart to peek out timidly. It is all too much to take in, especially when it has been so many years. A lot can happen in so many years.

She can't remember the last time she looked. Maybe she has never looked. How could she have never looked?

She is quite sure the quickest, most fluid motions of her body were made in the transition from bathed to clothed. She's had years of training. Tears well up in her eyes. Her shoulders sink forward and shake a bit as the tears fall. "I have grown accustomed to covering the messes," she admits, half in self-defeat and half in hopeful redemption, because although the messes are used to being covered, there is still life in her bones and still time to change.

She stares at the stranger who is sobbing awkwardly, the tears drip-dropping onto the bathroom counter below her. An occasional tear splashes on her still-curled toes. She releases her toes, stares at the chipped toe-nail polish through foggy eyes. She notices a few small black hairs on her big toe. She reaches for her razor and then stops. She tries to memorize the imperfect, splotchy skin with the ugly, small black hairs. She realizes if she doesn't memorize them, no one will.

Who exactly did she think was going to recognize this person in the mirror if she didn't? Who else would be patient enough to coax shoulders into place, smooth down crinkly gray hairs, or patch up the paint job on her toes? Who else would take the time to notice three little black hairs, sagging skin, or muscles that have emerged from hardship and determination?

She had thus far spent a lifetime of perfecting the seamless transition from dirty to clean, but she realizes that even the clean has never been clean enough. The fog on the mirror has been so convenient all these years.

You haven't looked because you haven't wanted to see. You haven't paid attention because you didn't want to know. You haven't liked yourself because you don't know yourself. And others don't know you.

She surprises herself with a smile in the mirror, her wet eyes lighting up with a glimmer. "I will love you when you're naked," she whispers to herself, leaning dangerously close to the mirror. "I will study your unedited bits. Your uncovered flaws. The darkness of your details. I won't be afraid to go there with you. And then I will lead you out of here. My buried soul, rescued. Your freedom is more important to me than anything in the world. I have lived with you and ignored you. Now I will pay attention and become familiar with your hidden beauty. There is still time."

We do have time. As long as we are still breathing, there is time. Time to give ourselves a chance. Time to let ourselves off the hook. Time to pay attention to the parts of ourselves that we've hushed up in an effort to make others happy.

When I was first married, I worked at a store in the mall. During my breaks I liked to explore. I would walk down to the mall drugstore and get a package of peanut-butter crackers and a bottle of juice, or a bag of mini-cookies and bottle of milk, and I would people-watch in the food court.

There was one lady in particular who got my attention. She had to be in her forties or early fifties. She had muddy blonde hair and a short stature, which was aided significantly by her extremely generous high heels. Her body looked a bit crowded in the middle, as if some things had sunk and other things had tried to rise up in anarchy, and they'd all reconvened midtorso. And she was bent, her back rounded, so that the top half of her body always arrived somewhere a good half second before the bottom half.

Her head was always down, focused with intensity on each step of the mall hallway before her. She wore tight, flashy clothing with low necklines and sequins that caught the light, beckoning attention, as if she needed any help. Her jean shorts—she always wore shorts—rode dangerously close to her aging curves, and as she clipped along in her aggressive pace, you would sometimes see the intensity of her tan line going from burnt orange to pale white along the base of her glutes. And in case you didn't happen to pick her out in the crowd, you could certainly count on being alerted to her presence by the pointing fingers or nudging gestures of others and follow their stares to watch her high-heeled prance through the retail speedway.

One day while I was working, my two coworkers and I saw her through the big glass store windows. They sneered and guffawed and called her a prostitute.

"Really?" I asked, wondering how I was too naive to miss that. "How do you know?"

They looked at me and then looked at each other and started laughing.

"Come on, Mandy. Isn't it obvious?"

"I mean, I know she dresses kind of provocatively, but so do a lot of people half her age, and you don't call them prostitutes."

"Well, she is one. I know a guy who got her number once. She just comes here to drum up business."

I still wasn't buying it. My coworker was lying, wasn't he? I was intrigued. What would it be like to meet a prostitute? Better yet, how awesome would it be to find out my coworker was wrong about her?

When my thirty-minute break came around, I decided the best thing I could do to ease my inquiring mind was to meet her. So off I went for my peanut-butter crackers and my bottle of juice from the mall drugstore, and then I waited at one of the major hallway intersections for her to come back around.

As she approached, I tried to fall in line beside her but was surprised by just how quick a pace she actually kept. Typically I enjoyed resting my sore legs during my breaks, but this break was going to be of a different nature entirely.

"Do you mind if I walk with you?" I asked, stretching my long legs out longer than my normal stride in order to keep up.

"No, I guess not." Her voice was soft, much more gentle and feminine than I expected. I thought her voice would be more aggressive to match her pace.

I could sense her discomfort, so I quickly explained that I worked in the mall and was on my break and that I'm always looking for an interesting way to pass my time. Her demeanor changed a bit, and I felt the invisible electric fence between us being turned off. Now I only had a scraggly barbed-wire fence to contend with. Would she warm up to me?

At this point, she hadn't yet made eye contact with me. The interesting thing is, she never would. Throughout our entire conversation she kept her makeup-thick eyes to the floor in front of her.

"So I see you here a lot," I said, trying desperately to make small talk and not embarrass myself by becoming noticeably winded.

"Yes, I come here to get exercise. I enjoy walking the halls. It's cool in the summers and warm in the winters," she said, her voice still sounding a bit suspicious of me.

"You're definitely getting exercise. You move fast! And I have to say, you're pretty brave to get your exercise in high heels. Why not wear tennis shoes?"

She chuckled, though her lips didn't give her away. The laughter slipped through quickly before her lips had a chance to lift into a smile.

"Because I like to dress nice. It's fun." She said it with such innocence, I felt as though I was walking with a three-year-old who was clopping down a tile hallway in her mama's shoes and makeup.

I began to notice we were being watched. People pointing, whispering, sniggering. I felt bold walking beside her, assuming her confident prance of a pace as my own. I wondered if she really could be a prostitute. If so, would she be approached by men while we were walking? Would she stop at some point and hand out business cards?

I asked what her name was and what she did for a living.

"Judy," she said. "I work at a country club. I'm a waitress. I usually have to dress in all white and black, so it's a nice change to come here and wear something more colorful."

Colorful indeed, I thought. Did she have any idea what people were saying about her? Did she know her tan line was showing?

We walked past the big glass windows of my store. I looked over Judy's head, waving to my coworkers, who looked as if they had just seen a ghost. They were shaking their heads and laughing.

"Do people ever say things to you? Make comments?"

"Oh, sure. Sometimes people laugh at me. I hear them." Her voice hesitated for a moment, cracking, but she gathered herself and continued, "It's not going to change what I do, though. I like my outfits. I like coming here to walk. I've just learned to put up with it."

Her words pulled on my heartstrings. We do learn to put up with a lot, don't we? I wondered if she had any friends to fight for her. I wondered if she always had to go it alone.

As my short break came to an end, I thanked her for letting me be her exercise companion.

"Maybe I'll see you again sometime. We're both here a lot."

"Yes," she said. "That would be nice." And I really think she meant it, though she still didn't look at me.

I exited her walking pace. It felt like that strange jolt you get when you step off an escalator, and all movement comes to an instant standstill.

I watched her walk away, seeing her with new eyes. Taking in her unedited bits and her uncovered flaws and the sketchy darkness of her details. She was messy. Maybe she *was* a prostitute, and she just totally played it off.

Regardless, my senses were telling me this was a woman doing her best to live fully alive. A woman trying to figure out who she was and have the boldness to live that out. A worn-down woman who'd had one too many punches thrown her way. Who had been flattened by one too many molds and was choosing to fight back one pair of tight, tattered jean shorts at a time. She was a woman who found herself worth fighting for, who was unashamed by the naked parts that everyone else kept pointing out and laughing over.

Perhaps the "Beware of God" T-shirts and two-toned tan lines aren't really to keep God away at all but are to keep the status quo away. The finger pointers. The people standing on the sidelines waiting to show us how we're doing it all wrong.

Perhaps the "Beware of God" T-shirts and the two-toned tan lines create a buffer, a cocoon of sorts, for the people who just want to live their lives uniquely but feel a bit claustrophobic going about it. Perhaps they think, *If I am odd to an extreme, maybe you'll just write me off as a crazy and leave me alone.*

Perhaps doing it a different way, your own way, isn't something to be ashamed of, even if people slap a label on you and call your naked-mirror moments a sleazy form of prostitution. Perhaps the road to the narrow gate is also paved with mall hall tiles and the reverberating sound of clicking high heels.

The alternative is being dutiful. I have played the role as dutiful. I would suspect that this is a role young girls are much more likely to play than young boys. I slipped right into the persona of the nice girl at a young age. Do not make waves, do not make mistakes, do not voice questions, and do not be angry. I can vaguely remember a conversation with a friend in junior high. It happened in a crowded hallway, in front of walls of lockers surrounded by mobs of chatty students. I was upset about something to the point of clenched teeth and stinging tears, a daily occurrence in junior high. My friend said, "What are you angry about?"

Without making eye contact, I replied in a cold, short voice, "I'm not angry. I'm just frustrated."

"You always say that, but you sure do look angry to me."

"Leave me alone," I said. "You don't understand."

I felt guilty for the emotion of anger. I felt guilty that I wasn't living the perfect life that everyone seemed to expect out of me and that I expected from myself. I walked around in a sort of bruised body, like many junior-highers do, waiting for the next blow to my self-esteem, all the time knowing that my religion would have me just believe harder in a God who prefers my good performance, so I could be saved from all this misery. The answer was always to do more good, and more good meant stuffing real feelings of inadequacy and dysfunction and even anger farther and farther down inside me.

It becomes really easy to learn the rules and play the game if you're interested in that sort of thing, which I was. Somehow the phase of rebelling passed me by, so tangled was I in the fear of disappointing anyone. I single-handedly wove a web of performance and then managed to get stuck in it.

I remember being in college, sitting on my bed in the shadows, sandwiched under my roommate's loft, gazing out the window to the back parking lot of my college dorm. I can remember the green-and-white, spiral-bound journal I was using at the time, writing out my apologies to a Jesus I just couldn't seem to satisfy. I didn't have time for the dramatic girls who were wasting their time experimenting with sordid things like cigarettes and sex and soap operas, skipping studies in exchange for drinks or romance or even just a quiet conversation at a coffee shop. I had a messy life, unchecked areas that must be put right. I felt a bit haughty with my green-and-white journal and my Jesus conversations furling around my mattress, my own modern-day equivalent to flogging.

When I was in grade school, I remember playing on a swing set in my friend's backyard. Every couple of minutes I would think up a new routine to do. Maybe this time I would climb up and do a flip over the top bar. Maybe this time I would swing hard and fast and then leap from the swing. Maybe this time I would slide down the slide on my feet. With each new creative twist, I would run into the house and ask Barb, my friend's mom, if I could have her permission to try the death-defying stunt. Time and time again, I would open the back door and ask for permission (or beg for forgiveness if I had attempted something for which I hadn't gotten her approval first). Eventually my in-and-out, in-and-out, in-and-out got to Barb, and she said, "Mandy, you can stop coming inside. Just go play. I trust you."

"But what if I get hurt? Or what if I do something I'm not allowed to do? Or what if I make you mad?" I inquired, fidgeting with my fingers in worry.

"That's just part of being a kid. Go play."

It would have been nice if, as a young adult, I could have heard those same words. I kept returning to meet Jesus in my sloppy bed, where the fitted sheet would inevitably slide off and reveal the harsh blues of my mattress, and I would frustratingly and embarrassingly rush to cover up the edges. I would return again and again and again to say, "But what about this, and what about that, and oh, did you see that horrible thing I did over here?" It was my confessional. My little bed booth where I could prove my unworthiness and beg Jesus to take me back on as a pro bono case.

I wonder why I never heard God say, "Mandy, you can stop coming inside. Just go play. I trust you." When I would scribble my lists of sins into the green-and-white spiral notebook, why did I never hear Him comfort me with, "That's just part of being a human. Go play"?

I was a sort of zombie, as I look back on it. A dead woman walking. Or maybe I was more like a marionette, each string pulled by a different person. I made a decision to settle for whatever it was that would keep the most peace.

Good Christians and good girls don't speak out of line. They don't question. They don't rebel. They don't rear up their little heads and scream, "But this is not the life I want for myself! Don't you see? This is not it at all." Good girls and good Christians, they suffer and sacrifice, and they do it all in silence, because this is the way of the cross or the way of the saint. But in my case, it was also the way of the empty.

Years went by, and I was still living my life as a marionette. It didn't end for me in college. How could it? There wasn't a defiant bone in my body. I had removed them all and sold them to the Devil so I could keep him happy as well. I rolled right into marriage with the same sort of mentality. I expected my husband to define who I was and how I should live. There were new rules to play by, and there were plenty of seasoned Christian women with the answers to give me when I needed advice.

Having no self-esteem is a frightful way to enter any relationship, but especially a marriage. I looked for value in all the wrong places. Let me be as flawless and beautiful and sexy as the women in pornography, because now, all of a sudden, this Christian girl, who claimed virginity as a prize for years, is supposed to flip a switch and be the sexual tigress of her husband's dreams. Where does one learn such skills?

Let me make your meals and clean your home and give you a massage and sit at your feet like a needy puppy dog, because you are my entire world now. You are it. There are no sports or grades to consume my achievements. I have my job and I have you. If you are ever upset, it's due to my failure, and if you ever want time apart from me, it's due to my character flaws. I own it all. The responsibility falls on my shoulders. It is too much to bear, but I will bear it anyway. Welcome to the life of a mad, dutiful Christian wife.

One night, within the first month or so of returning from our honeymoon, Tony told me he was going to go out with his friends.

"Out, like without me?" I asked, a bit panicked.

"Yeah. Well, that's what I was thinking. Just with the guys. Would that be okay?"

"Uh, I guess so," I said out loud, but all the while my insides were freaking out. There were words throwing themselves against the inner lining of my body, trying to force their way out, but I felt too timid to let them confess that I was feeling abandoned. I didn't know anyone in this town he had moved me to. How could he do this to me? Did this one act of entertainment mean he was choosing his college friends over me? Why would he not want me to tag along? Was I an embarrassment? Maybe it was my clothes. I needed to get new clothes. Or maybe it was the stupid things I would say in conversation. I bet it was my haircut. No, I bet it was my body. I should probably go running more often.

I resisted the urge to lunge across the floor and throw my arms around his ankles. "Don't leave me," I could scream, pathetically grasping for one last shot at my marriage before he disappeared into the fog of Friday-night men in sports bars who discuss all the lame things their women manage to do.

As you can tell, I was completely in control of my own imagination. Things weren't getting out of hand at all.

In many ways, I had an arguably good life. I know there are people, maybe people who are reading this book, who have all the same elements to their lives in place, only they are genuinely happy. Christian upbringing, churchgoing, Bible reading, and playing by the rules are certainly not signs of a life gone awry. For me, though, there was something going on deeper, beneath the surface. My motivations were skewed, and my heart wanted to please everyone at any cost. God was an ever-present, slightly perturbed janitor who had to keep mopping up my sins.

I love that bent-over, broken Mandy who would gladly bleed out in the effort to make anyone happy. She is me, even now. I think there is great wisdom in not divorcing our former selves or harboring regrets for the choices of our past. Life is a process, and I did the best I could do at the time. Hindsight just offers acute vision, and there have been layers of blindfolds removed from my eyes since that time. I am ever awakening, now at a speed so fast, it makes me nauseated if I look out at the blurring scenery through the window of the train of my life.

I look at my past with a microscope in the hope of understanding where I came from. I inspect closely, because that girl is so foreign to me now, I hardly even recognize her. The details, smooshed slimy between the glass slide and the plastic slide cover, are pretty ugly. But even ugliness, in the light of redemption, takes on great beauty.

I am in this glorious phase of unbecoming, of unlearning, of unschooling. I am peeling away residue from days gone by, freeing my mobility, cutting strings of the web I was stuck in and the strings to my marionette appendages. I am becoming a real girl, much like Pinocchio became a real boy. I'm learning that wishing on a star is far more valuable than I ever entertained.

Somewhere between marriage and kids, I reconnected with a love of art, a twinkling star I had long since stopped wishing on. I applied to grad school for graphic design, and to say I was disappointed when I didn't get accepted would be an understatement.

I wasn't used to being told no.

I sat across a desk from a clean-cut man dressed in black. His office was sleek, minimalistic. I drooled over the oversize Apple computer display and fantasized about my own little art studio. Stacks of art students' work surrounded us, taunting me as I nervously awaited his response to my portfolio.

"I'd like to see you spend some more time working on your portfolio and then reapply in a year or so." He broke the news to me quickly, and I could feel the wind suck out of my sails.

I am a proud achiever. I don't walk lightly into circumstances that I might fail at. I am a succeeder. I am actually surprised his response wasn't a nail in the coffin of my artist's heart. God must not want me to be an artist, right? He'd shut the door and locked it tight.

Thankfully, what happened instead is that this rejection lit a little flame inside me. Just a small blue flame, a pilot light. It was an angsty little flame that said, "I am not going to take no for an answer, and I don't need your stupid little school to validate me." It would take me a while, though, to have the courage to acknowledge that bold little rebellious voice as my own or to give it permission to speak out loud. I would flounder for the next five to seven years to find any semblance of my artistic voice, but I have that one quick exchange with a graduate professor to thank for the relighting of a flame, the reconnecting to a wishing star that would stir things to life in me, including spiritual things.

Although Tony and I didn't jump into having kids immediately upon marriage, it did happen about three years in, and though I was ready for it, I realize now that one can never really be ready for something new. It just must be entered into. No amount of words from friends, family, or even God Himself can prepare you for all you must walk through when it is new territory to walk. It is only through the walking that you learn to adjust to your new surroundings and make them your own.

From 2002 to 2008, we had four babies and two miscarriages. And if that wasn't enough, we made two big cross-country moves. My husband was battling what I believe to be depression, though there was never any clinical diagnosis, and I was flailing for the courage and space to call myself an artist. We were on parallel journeys, trying to find ourselves. At the time, the waters seemed so muddy and the ride seemed so bumpy, and yet it was all we knew. We believed in each other. We believed in our little family. We believed we were listening to God, but we had no tricks left in the bag to make the life we wanted come true. We felt beaten down, forgotten, ignored, passed over, stuck, and irritable.

I can remember walking outside our home with a screaming baby, our first, trying to give Tony some distance from the noise. He was working a job he despised as a beverage delivery man, and I can still picture him sitting on the floor in our family room, his legs spread wide with stacks of money and checks strewn on the carpet in between, pulling his hair out trying to make the calculations come out right.

As I walked on the narrow pathway surrounding our home, I bounced our little girl in my arms and let the tears fall to the rhythm of my bouncing. "This is not what I had in mind. This is not the life I thought I could offer you. This is not the life I wanted." I was apologizing to my newborn, but simultaneously I was apologizing to myself. Attempting to mother my own heart, as I realized how broken everything felt.

I took myself on many walks in those six transitional years. Some of them literal walks, some of them in my mind. In one walk I found myself sitting on the wall of a school playground, boys riding their bikes around me, yelling at each other playfully and dangerously throwing rocks at bees. I wondered if I'd get stung.

These walks were the chances to catch my breath amidst the chaos. Chances to try to get some space. But it's very hard to get space when you're in the hamster wheel, and it just keeps spinning. I wasn't sure how to exit the wheel gracefully. I wasn't sure how to find myself a quiet, compact, neon-orange plastic tube to hunker down in for a while to catch my breath.

I wasn't sure how to slow down, and what's more, I wasn't sure I wanted to. I was still stubbornly holding out that maybe if I just kept running hard, my balance would right itself, and everything would be okay. I was a nervous little hamster, twitching my nose in every little corner of my life, scurrying from this to that to make sure all my responsibilities were being maintained and to ensure everyone's happiness. I was so caught up in the details of our lives that I didn't even realize how close I was to my breaking point.

Then one day it happened. I threw my own rocks at the bees.

In one angry, flour-dust-cloud of a moment with my four kids (a moment I have officially named Angry Homemade Noodles), I forgot to keep my feet moving, and I was thrown viciously off the wheel, landing in a crumpled, hurting mess. A mess of guilt and fear and doubt and hope and anxiety and anger and fatigue. I didn't know I had been living my life simply to please others. I thought I had been following the rules and wise advice I'd been given in order to obtain that life to the full I'd been promised. I felt cheated by the system. When had the rules expanded to include so much territory that my little hamster feet couldn't keep up? It was the painful and enriching beginning of a life lived off the spinning wheel, a life of eye-to-eye contact with the naked girl in the mirror. The bees were swarming, and I had a lot of stone throwing to do if I was going to get free.

Chapter Five

Voice

This morning a question popped into my head with such fury I couldn't ignore it. It stood boldly before me, presenting itself as if it were a military officer reporting for duty. The question was, "Why does Satan want to convince us that listening to our voice is selfish? What does he stand to benefit from that?"

Now I don't understand all there is to know about evil, and I am certainly not going to offer a handful of Bible verses to back up this thinking, but supposing there is an enemy who wants to steal and kill and destroy, and supposing his clearest intent is to keep us from hearing from God, don't you think it would be a great tactic to get us to distrust our own voice? Not just our spoken voice, but that deeper inner voice from which all spoken words stir. The voice that some may call your heart or your soul. The voice that clings to hope. The voice that wants you to believe in you.

In the book *The Shack*, the Holy Spirit, named Sarayu, is having a conversation with the main character. She tells him, "You will learn to hear my thoughts in yours."[1] Think about it. How else do we hear from God? Most people I talk to have never heard the audible voice of God speaking to them. We say God "speaks" to us through the Bible, but even if this is so, isn't there something that moves *inside* of us, that resonates with the words we read, that meets us right where we are in our lives and makes an agreement with God? If we pray and receive answers, don't these answers pop into our heads and into our hearts; aren't they internal?

What do we mean when we say God lives inside of us? And if He truly does, then doesn't it stand to reason that there is a voice inside of us that is God's voice? Don't our desires and hopes and dreams get melded into His as He gives us new hearts, hearts that aren't so bent or twisted or broken? I think the opportunity for a new heart is available, and I think the option to listen freely to that heart and trust its voice is available, but I think there are few who manage to accept it or trust it.

I have been, for a long time, afraid to trust the voice. I am only now trying to unroll the tightly coiled barbed wire from around my heart. It's a wire ball made up of law after law after law. It's a wire ball that I want to believe someone else had a hand in crafting. Some enemy. I feel as though my religion has left me reliant on outside sources to connect with God. "Trust in the Bible more than you trust in God." That's what I feel I've been told. "Trust in laws and rules more than you trust in God." "Trust in other, wiser elders' interpretations of the Bible more than you trust in God." Do you know how many different interpretations of the Bible there are? Who can say which is right? Who can say which is wrong?

What I've been left with at age thirty-two is a faith that is scared to trust what God is personally telling me. A faith that is timid to believe that the voice inside of me could actually be the same voice of God speaking to me and through me. What if I could just let go of all the anxiety and rely on my instincts, trusting that those instincts are God-led?

What joy fills my soul at the thought, so much so that I feel the hotness rise up in my cheeks, and I look quickly over both my shoulders, embarrassed that someone might see my affair with such a free-spirited idea. I feel I am typing heresy. Am I espousing those new-age-like beliefs I've been warned about? Am I on that slippery slope they told me never to play on?

I waffle. Am I good and full of God? No, I am wicked and evil and self-seeking and self-gratifying. And just like that, the wedge has been placed between me and God. If I doubt His power inside me, then I am dependent once again on my erratic compulsions of laws and rules to get to Him. I am back to needing a religion that can save me if I just adhere to each and every commandment. I am back to square one.

It seems to me that all Satan—or the emptiness of our hearts—really needs is two lies: one, we can't trust God. This may mean convincing us that He doesn't even exist, or if He does exist, His heart isn't for us. And two, we can't trust ourselves. For a couple years of my life, I believed the first lie. I was angry with God, and I felt as though He was not to be trusted. But for the majority of my life, I have believed the second lie. It's a scary place to live. A place that lives in the weeds of people pleasing, because certainly someone must have the answer I need. Someone must be able to tell me how to get my relationship right with God. So I try out all sorts of regimens and disciplines, bouncing from one formula to the next in an effort to die to self and find God. And let me assure you, a part of myself definitely died, but I was no closer to God. I would get glimpses of Him, but they were always glimpses that beckoned me to stray from my plan, and I couldn't risk straying from the plan. Surely to do so meant that I would stumble into some big dark hole to be sucked away from God forever.

It was shortly before my Angry Homemade Noodles breakdown that I received some advice that I, of course, took to heart in an urgent attempt to make things feel right in my life. Living in the brand-new state of Oklahoma (a big change from California) and eight months pregnant with our fourth baby, I attended a little gathering of Christian moms. It was a time set aside to discuss questions about parenting. I was thankful for the chance to meet some new women, but I also went there with a question I needed answering.

As I look back on it, it wasn't so much that I needed an answer as much as I needed an answer I could trust. My own answer, which was stirring within me, didn't feel good enough. I was looking for someone to talk me out of it. At a lull in the evening, I got up the courage to ask my question. It went something like this: "I'm an artist. And I love creating, but I'm really having a hard time finding the time to do that while raising my kids. They are little--just five, four, and two, and of course, one on the way—and I'm just wondering, is this a season of my life where I'm going to have to give up art entirely?"

Now that I think back on it, I cringe that I was offering such a personal question up for debate in front of women I had never met before in my life. They didn't know me, they didn't know my history;

they didn't know my heart's desires. All they could see was a frazzled mom who was looking for some peace. I don't blame the woman who gave me the answer that she did. (Well, let's be honest, for a time I did blame her, but I realize now that I had no business asking her the question in the first place or putting so much weight on her response.) She was simply assessing the very little information I had placed before her and offering some advice.

Her advice was something to the effect of, "Well, you could see if your husband would give you some time away from the kids on a Saturday morning or for an hour here or there so that you could create. But you do have very little children, and soon four of them, and they do need you and your attention. They will take a lot from you. You might need to give up art for a while or do art projects that you can include your kids in."

Other ladies jumped in at this point, offering suggestions for crafts I could do with my kids. I wriggled in my seat. Why were Popsicle sticks, pipe cleaners, and Elmer's glue such revolting thoughts to me? Have I become an art snob? I smiled politely, wondering why I had come as I stepped back into the ugly-duckling down I had come to know as home. Why am I so different?

The woman continued talking. "It's not forever. It's just for a time. Eventually, when they're grown up a bit, you'll have a little more free time to do those sorts of things."

I remember a sort of sinking in my heart as she said it. A feeling of, *I knew that was the right answer. I knew I was selfish to think otherwise.* At the same time, I felt relieved because the decision had been made for me. Art was out the window, and I was a full-time mom. Suddenly I was completely free to devote all my time to my kids. I wouldn't have to attempt the mad balancing act anymore. I was all theirs, just for a season, of course.

I think it was about two weeks after having baby number four, and in the throes of some sort of postpartum depression, that this season of sacrificing myself completely for my family ended with my being launched from my hamster wheel in a huff of anger.

We were making noodles, homemade noodles, for Thanksgiving. We were mixing eggs and flour and water, and things were going along nicely. I was feeling pretty accomplished as a mom, like our little home belonged on some perfect prairie. But within minutes, that picture was shattered. Kids began to fight and squabble, the newborn resting in the sling close to my body decided to let out an ear-piercing scream to announce his hunger. My hands were covered in noodle dough. I wasn't even halfway done, and my kitchen looked like a bomb had gone off. This wasn't what I had in mind for beautiful holiday traditions. My breathing became labored, my armpits sweaty, my cheeks flushed, and my milk let down. I felt more akin to the cow on the prairie than the elegant and patient mama.

This is it? This is life? I seek out God. I search, flailing, for the answers about how to live in a way that makes Him happy and therefore, hopefully, makes me happy. I give up art. I fully embrace this motherly role, and this, *this* is what I get?

I screamed. I yelled. I threw a tantrum in the clouds of flour, and I launched a rolling pin, hoping it hit the ghost of God on its way through. I told my kids what a horrible job we were doing at making noodles. I told them they had messed up everything. I looked at their big, blinking, empty blue stares, and I hissed at them, "Why do you need me all the time? Why can't you just be content?"

But inside I knew I was the one who wasn't content. Inside I was asking God, *Why do You need me all the time? You're asking too much of me. Would You just leave me alone?*

Inside I was crushed because I believed I'd messed everything up. And underneath that layer, I knew there was a layer that thought it was God who had messed everything up.

I sat on the floor and rested my head against the wall. I nursed my baby, not bothering to clean the dried noodle dough off my hands. I loathed my messiness, my crustiness, my failed attempts. I felt depleted, as if every suck my newborn took was draining the air out of me, and when Tony came home he'd find a wrinkled, empty balloon on the floor blowing around every now and then in the breeze of the ceiling fan. My kids would ask him, "Daddy, do you think you could blow Mommy up again?"

Can You put the air back into my lungs again?

There was so much turbulence inside. I was tired of fighting off the waves of questions. I had no energy left to fight. I was off the hamster wheel, and I felt myself relaxing, letting the waves toss me where they willed. Rising up and sinking back down, my toes barely scraping the sandy bottom. I wondered what mysteries were buried under the surface of the water. I was being pulled out to sea. The sea of the unknown.

It would take time, but I was ready to listen to the voice within. I had exhausted every other voice within my reach, and none of them seemed to have an answer as specific and finely crafted as I needed. What if the voice I really needed was the one echoing in my own chambers? Was that God's voice, or was it my own? Could those voices be merged into one?

Chapter Six

Running

Why do I fight against what I want so much? Why do I convince myself my desires are wrong or silly or impossible? Why do I have to be the one to talk myself out of something before anyone else does?

I distinctly remember a trip to meet my husband's grandparents for the first time. Tony and I hadn't been dating long. Maybe a month. Maybe even less. We spent some time visiting with them, and when it was time to leave, they wrapped their arms around me in a tight hug and told me they loved me. I am sure I must have hugged them like a fish, my arms limp at my sides, patting them a few times with my little fins so they knew I was alive. I looked at Tony over their shoulders, my eyes wide with surprise and confusion. He smiled, apparently enjoying watching me squirm with discomfort. His grandfather told me I was beautiful, told Tony what a lucky man he was and to take care of me. I didn't know whether I would blush or suffocate first; the room felt strangely out of air.

For the hour-and-a-half ride home, I contemplated what had just occurred. I was baffled by a love that was bold and unashamed and blind. "They don't even know me," I kept repeating to Tony. "How could they love me?" He seemed humored by my confusion, but I was not amused.

We hadn't been dating for that long; how could they say such a thing? What if it didn't work out between Tony and me? The "I love you" and hugs felt as though I had sealed the deal on a bargain I wasn't even aware we were making. Who exactly is it they love? Who do they expect me to be? What if I can't live up to that? What if I want out and break Tony's heart? Would I then be breaking his grandparents' hearts too? I felt trapped.

At the very same time, a part of me wanted to settle into the affection. I *was* enjoying my relationship with Tony. I enjoyed our conversations. His hand on mine made my heart race. His eyes were deep pools of blue that begged me to trust him. And I wanted to; I just wasn't sure if I could or should. It felt strangely good to have his grandparents' vote of trust. To know they approved of me enough to let Tony know he better hold on to a good thing. Maybe he would listen. Maybe they could convince him to never leave me or hurt me. Maybe I could get used to being called *beautiful* and settling into a warm embrace that said, "There is a place for you here. You belong."

It was a hot summer evening as we walked hand in hand, kicking up the dust along the outer lanes of our little hometown county fair. The sun was setting, leaving the sky with an orange-and-pink cast, and the air was thick with the smell of funnel cakes, sweat, and cigarettes.

"I asked Tom how you know if you love someone. How you know when you're ready to say the words *I love you*," Tony said to me, staring at the ground as we walked.

Tom was a good friend, a trusted confidant of Tony's. In fact, we had Tom to thank for arranging our first meeting. Had it not been for him, it's likely our two worlds never would have collided.

As Tony talked, I could feel my mouth get dry and my fingertips turn tingly. Was this going to turn into a real-life version of *Grease*, my own summer-lovin' moment, minus the black leather and big hair? Was he basically divulging to me, "You're the one that I want"?

It all felt too good to be true, and I knew if anyone had enough information on the reality of the situation, it was I. I couldn't let him or his grandparents make a mistake they would regret. I couldn't let them fall in love with someone I wasn't. And I believed, at the time anyway, that I wasn't beautiful, lovable, or worth keeping around. I saw myself more as an inconvenience, and I wasn't about to put myself in the awkward position of having them find out the truth of me after we all had given too much of our hearts away to one another. I wanted space and distance so I wouldn't disappoint anyone.

I remember having a conversation with my dad about dating.

"I think I'm done," I'd told him. It was my senior year of high school, prior to my meeting Tony.

"You're not done. You're just hurt. But love sometimes hurts."

He reminded me of the saying, "Better to have loved and lost than never to have loved at all."

I pondered it hard, but I just wasn't sure. I kept telling myself, *You're too vulnerable, Mandy. You give too much away. Your love is too raw.*

"I'm tired of loving people with my whole heart and then being abandoned. I give too much of myself away, and I think I'm done. I don't want to hurt like this anymore. It's not worth it. I don't want to ever get married. I'm going to be a nun."

I was so adamant about this, I had a good friend draw up a declaration of intent on a high school cafeteria napkin. "I, Mandy Pfeifer, will not ever get married. And in the event that I do, I vow to give Phil Sobers my ring finger." I signed my name to it, and two of my friends signed as witnesses.

On my wedding day, I unwrapped a little jewelry box from Phil. In it was the folded paper napkin that he had kept for nearly four years, a gracious gift to me as a wedding present. He told me I could keep my finger.

Thankfully, in dating Tony, I was love struck, and I couldn't carry out a decision to completely walk away. I kept telling myself he was different from the other guys I had dated—and he was. Our personalities weren't really of the "mess around" sort. As firstborns, neither of us had much patience for spending any time on something we weren't serious about.

I was caught up in the romance and the heartfelt conversations Tony and I exchanged. I had enough curiosity to stick around to see if perhaps this whole thing might be possible on some level, but I would still interject to Tony now and again that I had plans to live in a convent someday.

Exactly six short months after our first date, Tony secretly asked me to marry him. He hadn't planned on asking me that day. He didn't have a ring. It just sort of wonderfully happened.

We were young, just freshmen in college, and we hadn't known each other for long. I was still verbally committed to never getting attached to anyone, but my heart had made quite a different commitment. When he asked me to marry him, I couldn't even say yes with my mouth; I merely nodded. I was a timid little thing, unsure of what I was getting myself into, but too in love to stop myself. I was serious about Tony, and I hoped this meant he was serious about me. My trust-o-meter was on the fritz, so I had to go with my gut feeling.

As Tony and I sat on a couch in a dimly lit room of his parents' home, giddy over our secret engagement, I began to divulge to him all the truths I felt might convince him otherwise.

"You need to know some things about me," I started. "Some things that might make you think twice."

He was, I think, again humored by my discomfort. I continued with a list that sounded like it went on forever. "I cry a lot. I get hurt easily. My heart is wounded. I'm awkward. I'm scared of clowns. I hate math ..."

Tony interjected some imperfections of his own. "I have a temper. I speak my mind."

As we went back and forth, I believe we were both acutely aware that the exchange wasn't making us question our commitment, but rather was making us all the more committed. I was in love with his imperfections, and he was in love with mine. Two imperfect people pledging their love despite it all. That's how I remember spending the evening, cuddled up on the couch, embraced in another hug

I desperately needed but innately wanted to squirm away from. I wondered if love would always feel like such a paradox to me.

Fast-forward to this week, some thirteen years later. I felt drawn to watch a movie I hadn't watched in years called *Bed of Roses*.[1] In an instant that I can't explain, I knew I was supposed to watch it, and I knew I was supposed to think of the main male character, played by Christian Slater, as if he were God pursuing me.

I watched the movie with a journal on my lap and a pen in my hand, scribbling all sorts of phrases and insights that offered clarity to my current place in life. I watched the main female character as if pieces of my own life were playing out before me. Sure, she wasn't married with children, but she did have this great capacity for accomplishment and a large distrust for things like rest and intimacy. There was no time in her life for fun or romance or fantasy; she had things to do, and those things were grounded deeply in reality. I watched as she fought off a relationship that seemed too perfect. I listened as she said to her best friend, "I don't have time in my life for great. I work for a living, and I'm good at my job. He's wasting it on the wrong person."

I got tears in my eyes as he said to her, "You just can't admit that someone could love you." And my heart sank as I resonated with her realization that she had "nothing to give" in return for his love. She got scared off by the very thing she wanted most, because certainly if he could love her, he must not know her well enough.

"I didn't mean to scare you," he says to her, realizing that maybe his love was too intense, too much too quickly. "Just don't run away," he says, hopefully. But she does. She does run away. Back to her job, back to performance, back to life by her terms and under her control. Back to where it's safe.

The whole time I want to scream at her, "No. Don't go. This is what you want. He'll be patient with you. You can figure your relationship out as you go along. Just commit." But she doesn't hear me, and quite frankly, I realize I'm just like her, and I'm not hearing my own words or my own heart either. How can I see it so clearly for this woman in the movie and not see it for myself? I'm hoping this realization is a good place to start.

I have lived my life, thus far, performing, and I have done a great job at it. I have followed the rules of my religion. I have gone to church. I have read my Bible. I have made life changes when held accountable to do so. I didn't get pregnant as a teenager. I have served my husband and my kids. I have tithed 10 percent. I have served ministries and shared my faith. I have participated in fundraisers for good causes. I have been good at my "job," and as the main character's best friend states in the movie, "No one disputes this." I have done all this so that God would love me. I haven't necessarily loved this sort of life, but sacrifices aren't always something to love. What's important is not the joy in my heart but the completion of the task.

This is why I am thrown off when people want to interrupt my work to give me a hug and tell me they love me. I don't have time to exchange affection. I've got to keep my plates spinning. I don't know who I am apart from performance. Separate me from my performance, and I'm floundering, a fish out of water, flopping on the beach as sand awkwardly collects on my scales.

In the past two years, God and I have had some very intimate moments together when I have managed to let down my guard and let Him make me smile. I have read beautiful literature and found

Him in its midst. He has given me the new name of Artist, and the vision and purpose and confidence to try new things under my new name. He has sat with me through anger and allowed me to vent. He has released me from certain responsibilities so I might have room to breathe. He has asked me questions about my heart and given me time to explore answers. And I have walked timidly into it all, looking over my shoulder every now and then for the "catch."

But as I watched this movie, I realized the real test is in meeting His family, and this is the part where I relate so completely in the character's desire to just run away. It's one thing to have Him quietly and privately woo me and believe in me, like being engaged in secret. It's quite another thing to have Him affirm me in front of others as someone He loves and delights in.

I am in the painful process of watching these two worlds collide. My hidden fantasy of God speaking to me personally, and my nauseating introduction of this relationship to the world outside. How can His family, the church, possibly accept me? They don't even really know me. I beg of Him, "Let me return to the world of performance, where I pray before I eat, solely so other Christians know I love You. Let me watch kids in the church nursery so I can prove my devotion to You. Let me guard my tongue and say only kind, good, joyful things so they know You complete me, and I lack for nothing. Let me say sweet words to my kids and not pursue work outside of caring for our home, so they know I'm sold out to a good cause. Let me quote Scripture or hint that I had a devotional time with You earlier this morning, so they'll know of my commitment to You."

"You've come too far to return to that sort of living," He reminds me, and I know He's right. I've read Galatians far too many times now to kid myself into believing that my life to the fullest is wrapped up in proving myself to God or to His family. There is no longer life there for me.

I won't run away from You, God. Let me just run away from Your family. Much like the girl in the movie, I plead, "Can't we just have a private Christmas celebration at home, together, just the two of us? Why do we have to meet Your family?"

I sense that He gets this. He understands how hard it is for me to stand before them, not knowing what each of them expect from me.

Perhaps this family member won't approve of my foul mouth, which has developed as of late while I work through my anger issues.

Perhaps this family member won't approve of the glass of wine I sip on as I melt into His love and grace.

Perhaps this family member won't understand why I can't be in church right now.

Perhaps this family member will expect me to put my art on hold for the sake of my God and my family.

Perhaps this family member will disapprove of the way I talk to Him.

Perhaps this family member will disapprove of the way I dress, spend my money, or manage my time.

Perhaps this family member will think I'm being lazy.

Perhaps this family member will think I'm a bit presumptuous in the way I flaunt my love for Him or the way I presume to say He shows His love for me.

Perhaps this family member will want more of my time than I'm willing to give.

Perhaps this family member will think I'm not giving God enough of myself.

All I see are a bunch of foreboding eyes staring me down, and I don't know which ones to trust. Which ones will believe in me? Which ones will chastise me?

And so I just want to run away. Maybe I *am* just making this whole thing up. Maybe it *is* just a bunch of fantasy. Maybe this dream relationship I'm wishing for and seeing unfold, where God loves me as I am and woos me with the things that stir me personally, maybe it really *is* just a big selfish hoax. A daydream at best. Maybe I am just creating God in my own image, the way I'd like Him to be.

It's far easier to dismiss this than to believe in a love this big. It's far easier to abandon this than to defend myself to Your family. After all, they are Your family. They will protect You at all costs.

Recently my oldest daughter was having a tough morning with her siblings. I was in my room behind a closed door, where I go to find a wee bit of serenity to do my yoga practice. I had just finished the hard workout and was lying flat on my back on my yoga mat, calming my breathing. My head was close to the door, and I heard her sitting in the hallway crying. "What's wrong?" I whispered, pressing my lips close to the bottom of the doorframe so she could hear me. She told me her sister and brothers didn't love her.

I stood up slowly to avoid having the blood rush out of my head and walked to my nightstand. I opened the drawer and found a pencil and a piece of junk mail. I ripped off a blank edge of paper and wrote these words: "I will send you love letters under the door that tell you how much I love you."

I slipped it to her, and I heard her gasp with glee.

She sent me one back. It simply said, "Cool."

Her tears stopped.

My own tears started. I felt that burning sensation that happens in my nose, seconds before the welling up of tears in my eyes. I felt God saying to me, "This is what I do for you."

And I know He's right. As I go through my days, and I feel that ugly-duckling down of the unloved trying to smother me, I feel Him emerge, slipping love under doors, reminding me, *You're a swan. You're a swan. You're a swan.*

Little love notes that sometimes I can't be sure were from God or me doing something kind for myself. But does it matter? If I'm able to feel love now when the unloved moments hit, I don't care if I'm confused about its source. God is love, so wherever love flocks to, He must be a part of it.

I give myself a chocolate.

I see golden light hit my dining room wall in splashes, there for a moment and then gone.

A morning covers me warmly in a cocoon of thunder and lightning and dark mystery so I can write down haunting words in safety.

A friend gives me a new journal.

A new friend invites me to a yoga class at the exact studio I've been wanting to explore. I tell her, "You know, I don't think I believe in coincidence."

He's passing me love letters. *Am I reading too much into this?*

A friend surprises me and buys my food. How could she have known I couldn't really afford to eat out tonight?

A friend suggests a movie to me, and the script holds phrases I've been saying in my head but have never voiced to a single soul. I find a pen on the floor of the movie theater and use it to write down quotes and thoughts during the movie. I know it's a magic pen.

I carve out luxurious moments to read a book.

I hear a song that breaks me open.

He's passing me love letters. We're whispering under doors, our lips close so we can hear each other.

You're scaring me, God, with Your outrageous love, with Your promises of life to the full, with Your tastes of romance. You're scaring me, and You're putting me in a pretty tight spot, because I'm a confused and angry woman right now who doesn't know who she is but who desperately wants to believe that I actually am who You are saying You are in love with. I don't have any of myself left to give You. I'm a messy, crusty, deflated balloon covered in noodle dough. I'm nothing but a shaky little man behind a green curtain, pretending the smoke and fire is my actual persona. What happens when everyone finds out I'm not as wonderful as You're telling me I am? Then what?

Chapter Seven

Illiterate

In 2008, just short of one year after my Angry Homemade Noodles moment, I wrote a blog post about my hang-ups with reading the Bible. I've included the majority of that post below.

I don't want to read the Bible. I haven't wanted to for the past month at least. I've had minute efforts at picking it up and perusing it, but they are empty and merely guilt-induced. It feels dead to me.

Note what I'm not saying. I'm not saying, "God feels dead to me." Oh no. On the contrary, *He* feels very much alive. But at the risk of sounding heretical and sacrilegious, *He* feels bigger to me than the Bible. I've thought about this a lot, and I think what I mean by that is He feels bigger than what has become my religion. He feels bigger than quiet devotional times, Scripture memorization, and Sunday-morning churchgoing. He feels bigger than prayer time,

Christian music, and the polished "right" answers for life's hardest questions. I feel God wooing me, but it's oddly outside of all the traditional Christian venues I have known Him to speak through. It's as if my familiarity with Christianity is breeding contempt, and I'm not sure what to do about it.

I've been reading *The Sacred Romance*. This was written by John Eldredge, who was also a professor of mine my last semester of college. His "lectures," for lack of a better word, brought my faith to life again during my college years. And since I am now feeling a sort of dryness, I returned to the book that once before gave me a fresh perspective.

> There comes a place on our spiritual journey where renewed religious activity is of no use whatsoever. It is the place where God holds out his hand and asks us to give up our lovers [mine would be busyness, control, discipline, competency, perfection, etc.] and come and live with him in a much more personal way.... We are both drawn to it and fear it. Part of us would rather return to Scripture memorization, or Bible study, or service—anything that would save us from the unknowns of walking with God....
>
> [But] if we listen to our heart again, perhaps for the first time in a while, it tells us how weary it is of the familiar and the indulgent.[1]

I have a deep desire, and I believe a Holy Spirit–directed longing, to try something different and to change things up in my life.

I'm tired of my routine, tired of being in the rut I've somehow gotten stuck in, tired of the box I've kept God in.

Most recently, there was the realization that I heard God loud and clear through reading the novel *Frankenstein,* by Mary Shelley. Not exactly your typical reading material for biblical truth.

And it's happened in other areas of my life too. Every Friday this summer, our family has gone to see a movie, and I have heard God's voice loud and clear through these stories:

Nim's Island

Kit Kittredge

Kung Fu Panda

The Tale of Despereaux

I feel God's peace when I smell my baby's head. I feel God's love when my husband puts his hand on me warmly and whispers a prayer over me before leaving for work in the morning (especially after we've been arguing over stupid stuff). I feel God's creativity when I stroke paint colors onto a canvas or see just the right colors mix together in the kitchen or in an outfit my kids wear.

I am being romanced, and I'm baffled by the fact that it isn't directly coming from the Bible or the church building. I think God is chasing me. I think He is sensing my distaste for the mundane and recognizing that my heart is waning, so I think He's coming after me in the things that are speaking to my heart right now.

I love a God who is bigger than human religion.

I had a professor in college who advised me once about praying before meals. I didn't understand why it was necessary and why everyone did it, and yet I kept doing it because I felt like I should. I felt guilty not doing it. It must be necessary to be a Christian, I figured. He advised me to stop doing it. Why do something if I was only doing it out of guilt?

So I've decided I just need to outwardly confess that I'm not reading the Bible right now. I'm taking a break. I am taking a chance. I'm obeying, I believe, and choosing to hear God where He is speaking to me right now. I'm trying to fight off guilty feelings and resting in the fact that even when I try, I'm ultimately not in control. It feels good to be real with these feelings and to stop pretending the Bible is doing anything for me right now. Isn't life messy? I'm just glad my heart feels like living it again.

Where are You taking me, God? You sure are unpredictable.

As I look back, a year and a half later, on my confusion and frustration with the Bible, I realize my main problem was over-saturation. Too much of a good thing. I have spent thirty years living with the Bible. I have been raised in communities where those words are memorized, preached, taught, and believed without question. I have been in such close proximity to them, I can't even appreciate their beauty. It's as if I am viewing a beautiful painting with my nose pressed up against it. Sure I see things, but my vision is blurry at best, and my head feels a bit dizzy from the close inspection.

I recently had the opportunity of speaking at an intimate artists' gathering at a church in Colorado Springs. After I finished talking, the floor was opened up for questions and discussion. A man by the name of Joe shared with me a discussion he'd had with a fellow artist. He said he believed we were entering a second Renaissance.

"In the first Renaissance," he said, "God used the likes of Michelangelo to convey His message to an illiterate people. The people did not read or write and God reached out to them. It was through this expression that these artists are now seen as the equivalent of today's rock stars in the art world. Today, in this impending second Renaissance, God is once again going to use the arts, but now it will convey His message to an illiterate church."

I was taken by his words *illiterate church.*

Yesterday I was talking to a Christian woman, and in the course of our discussion, she brought up Bible reading.

"I just think maybe if I was in a small group with other Christians, I'd be forced to read my Bible," she said. "Because I'm going to be honest, right now I'm not reading it. I'm not reading it at all." I could tell she felt a bit humiliated by admitting that.

Wouldn't it be better if we desire to read the Bible so much that we do it on our own? I thought to myself.

I pushed back. "But why would you want to be forced to do something you don't want to do?"

"Because I think I may need it," she said.

"Okay, well that's fair. If you feel like your life is legitimately missing something. I just know I've struggled personally with feeling guilt over something *the church* is asking me to do, versus feeling internally like it was really something *I* wanted to do."

"Sometimes I think you have to do the action in order to work your way into the desired feeling."

I pondered this. It felt a lot like "fake it till you make it" to me, a phrase that makes me cringe. But she did have a point. I certainly felt that way with exercise. I want a desired outcome of fitness, but I rarely feel like I want to exercise. I do it because I want the end result, not because the idea of it seems pleasant at the time. But this wasn't really faking it, was it? As my friend Lori once said to me, "It's not about authenticity but about choice." So maybe this woman knew from past experience that Bible reading, for her, produced an end result that she desired. Maybe it was a choice she desired making as a means to an end.

For me, I don't feel like I'm missing anything being away from the Bible. There have been times in my life when the Bible has impacted me, but now when I read the words, they sound hollow. Now I'm finding interaction with and revelations from God in the more nontraditional paths I spoke of. My intimacy with the Divine is intact, even if my Bible reading has waned for a season. The woman I spoke to sounded as if she was missing interaction with God entirely, and she felt as though church community and Bible reading would rebirth that in her. We are all so different, aren't we?

I read a blog post last week that posed the questions, "How do you make sure you're reading the Bible? What does your Bible reading plan or schedule look like?" I jumped at the opportunity to share where I was with all that. I left this comment:

> This is a discussion that is near and dear to my heart. The skin is still fresh on the wound of this splinter that I had to go deep to dig out. Bible reading, quiet time, or whatever the Christian sect calls it, has been

a splinter in my faith for years. For a time I had to stop reading the Bible altogether to detox from the legalism it personified for me. Then I read Galatians for a year off and on, trying to grasp the idea of no need to work for grace. Finally I'm inching my way back into reading the Bible, but it is solely on an "I want to do this" basis. If there is even a twinge of "I'm reading this out of guilt or because I'm trying to live up to the proper Christian standard," my Bible does not get opened. I refuse to read what I believe are meant to be life-giving words in that context of legalism. And the strangest thing and scariest thing to say is I really believe God is okay with my choice to engage with the Bible in this way. I am healing. These things take time and lots of space. I may never read the Bible consistently again. Who knows? What I do know is I have peace and joy in my life again, and I feel closer to God than ever before. My faith feels adventurous and alive. A great trade-off for the years of guilt-induced Bible reading plans and dutiful quiet times.

It felt good to speak freely and openly about my journey with this, especially since a year and a half ago, I cringed at admitting on my blog that I was taking some time off from Bible reading. So much guilt, and it felt so good to let go of it.

I returned a couple of times to this blog post to read the conversation that was unfolding through the comments, but I was disappointed to find that many people were posting about the rules they use for making sure they read their Bible or their Bible reading plan of choice and how they had fallen off the wagon in years past, but this year they were going to redouble their efforts to read the Bible every day.

I felt angry. Angry that I had written my pure, unedited, even vulnerable thoughts and had thrown them out in the midst of a discussion that had turned so legalistic in nature. I felt angry that there seemed to be a sort of Bible reading competition waging in the blog discussion. I felt angry that very little was said about connecting to God Himself. *Illiterate*, I thought. *They are missing the point entirely.* Why are we all missing the point entirely? Whom can I point a finger at to blame for this guilt-induced way we approach the Bible? I didn't know where to point my anger. I decided it was best if I didn't return to read any more comments. My heart was just not ready to go there.

With a little space from that blog conversation, I realized there is no one person to blame. It's quite possible, in fact, that the people leaving comments didn't even have a problem with legalism or feeling like the Bible was dead. Maybe they really were honestly excited about Bible reading plans, and maybe these Bible reading plans really did help them connect with God in a satisfying way. Maybe they were just like the Christian woman I had a conversation with yesterday. Who was I to assume? Who was I to transpose my issues onto their lives? Maybe the path to the narrow gate can be walked on by both Bible lovers and Bible illiterates. Maybe both can find life to the full.

So I return to me, to where *I* am. I return to the reason I am writing this book in the first place, so I can sort out my own life and the reasons I want to be living it fully. And there I'm reminded that life to the full, for me, isn't ever about words read because I'm told to read them.

Or words read because I'm told God will mainly show Himself to me there.

Or words read because they are promised to be life itself.

Because life to the full for me isn't about pretending, and if the truth is going to set me free, what am I doing pretending instead of being truthful about how empty I feel with my little leather Bible open because someone told me, "You'll do it if you really love Him"? Life to the full requires me to be honest, and the truth of the matter is I feel condemnation and boredom and confusion and pressure when I flip through the pages of the Good Book.

I don't know why exactly that is. If it's because I've read the words too long, or because I've had others interpret them for me in ways they were never meant to be interpreted, or because I've had a taste of a living God that's giving me new revelations. A God who surprises me by interacting with me in very personal ways throughout my everyday life that I'm just not accustomed to. I don't know. But I'm tired of pretending, especially in a relationship with someone I love so dearly. And I'm tired of thinking He's going to condemn me simply because I'm not following the rules. I'm exhilarated when I see His biblical truths of love and life to the full and freedom and light and magic and power and hope and belonging show up through novels and movies and music and nature and people who haven't been deemed worthy and overlaid with that all-protective label of *Christian*.

I'm not claiming to be in a place of great health. I readily admit my bouts of anger that have no clear direction or purpose. I readily admit there are moments when I think I might just be going crazy. But may I assure you, as I'm assuring myself, that these are not the moments when I'm sitting with Him. These are not the moments when my mind is still. These are the moments when I'm running helter-skelter, bouncing from one people-pleasing notion to the next, trying to live up to some standard I've had modeled for me, some mold I believe it's my duty to force myself into. For when I sit with Him, I feel sanity and peace. I feel wholeness and love. I feel light despite a darkness of the unknown. And I feel that He is with me, showing me how wonderful it is that He is bigger than I presumed.

Chapter Eight

Darkness

There is a novel titled *My Name Is Asher Lev* in which the young Jewish boy, who is a budding artist, has an internal struggle over light and dark. His mama repeatedly asks him throughout the book to "make the world pretty" with his drawings, because "it's nice to live in a pretty world."[1] But Asher is acutely aware that the world isn't always pretty. That sometimes the dark places have to be acknowledged to set something free inside yourself, and without the awareness and contrast of the dark, the light isn't nearly as beautiful.

One day he draws a picture of his mama, and upon finishing it, he pauses and then looks around desperately. Finally his eyes land on an ashtray of cigarette butts. He lunges for one, using it to add much-needed shading to his mama's face.[2] Later he explains to his papa, "I wanted to draw the light and the dark."[3]

There is a certain danger that comes with darkness, but lately I am in a place in my life where I cannot ignore the dark anymore. I need it as much as I need the light. My soul is buried down deep inside me somewhere, shivering in fear, and I've got to dive in and find it and rescue it. I'm like Despereaux, the puny little mouse in Kate DiCamillo's book *The Tale of Despereaux*,[4] suited up with my spool of red thread and my needle sword, and I'm willingly entering the dungeon by my own choice to save a princess I know is imprisoned in the depths below.

It occurs to me, as I'm tiptoeing down the dungeon stairs, that I haven't been honest with myself. I'm realizing that truth isn't just what I wish existed. Truth is what really exists and that is both darkness and light. I wonder if this half-truth living is a life lived on the wide road, a life that is half full.

I wonder, too, as I rub my hand along the clammy, cold stone of the walls leading down to the dungeon, if by chance I will never escape out of the dark. Perhaps I will be swallowed by the beasts I must face. Or maybe I will become one of them to survive. Will my eyes become so accustomed to seeing the dark side of things that I'll forget the light?

Somewhere I have gotten it in my mind that God knows nothing of the dark. That God hangs out in the golden light of heaven, where all is beautiful and shiny and perfect, and that He would prefer me to be there as well. That what it means to be a Christian is to paint pretty pictures because we have a Savior who already went into the depths of darkness to free us. Isn't it so wonderful and happy and joyous? Isn't it so perfect and pristine and put together, this Christian life?

One Saturday evening I was at church with my family. Tony and I were standing, along with everyone else, for the worship music. But this night, they did something different. They broke from singing midsong and, while the band continued to play, the pastor started reading off the prayer request cards. He read about a woman with cancer, about a man suffering from depression, about a couple in financial crisis. And as he read, I felt as if I was seeing dark and light intermingling.

Afterward, I felt I needed to express my thankfulness for the revelation I had received, so I went up front to talk to the pastor.

"Typically the worship is so polished and perfect that I feel as though God is unapproachable. It feels like the room is being overpowered with light, which is great, but tonight, tonight there was this new depth, because suddenly the hurts and hang-ups of people, the real, messy dark stuff we deal with as humanity, were being revealed right in the midst of all that lightness. It was powerful and welcoming."

"Thanks for letting me know," he said, and then added, smirking, "You're one of those weird artist intuitive types, aren't you?" We both laughed.

Later I wondered, is there something weird about my liking that mix of light and dark? Is this a narrow-road mentality that few would agree to? Would most people want church to be all light? Would most people want their pastor to just paint pretty pictures?

I have spent my life feeling as though my faith must be lacking because the light is just not enough for me. Being leery to admit that there is a princess rumbling inside me, longing to get out. Jesus may have saved her, but I still don't feel free. Why don't I feel free? I've been told it's because I don't read my Bible enough or sacrifice enough or pray enough or memorize Scripture enough.

But could it be possible that I have a part to play? That I have my own darkness to contend with? That if I am ever going to be open to the power of this divinity that supposedly dwells within me, I'm going to have to be open to playing with fire in the underbelly of darkness? Could it be that I have my own battle to fight, and that Jesus's sacrifice was to give me access to the power I would need to fight it?

Maybe He isn't hurt by my admittance of the world not being all pretty, even if it is His world. Maybe He isn't ashamed or fearful of my journey into the dark. Maybe He has been waiting for me to take it all along, wondering if I'd ever sneak away from the light, trusting it was necessary for my soul's survival. Maybe He knows of darkness more than any of us. He is one step ahead of us, dotting the black with stars, illuminating our moons so that even in the deep black, we may have access to light.

I love how Madeleine L'Engle even contends that there is a dark side to the divine:

> It is a frightening thing to open oneself to this strange and dark side of the divine; it means letting go of our sane self-control, that control which gives us the illusion of safety. But safety is only an illusion, and letting it go is part of listening to the silence, and to the Spirit.[5]

This darkness I consider myself to be in presently is where I'm becoming aware of my monsters. I'm seeing the huge looming shadows and hearing the slithery sounds at my feet. It's scary to face the addiction to performance and perfection and people pleasing. It's scary to see that somehow the light had in some ways blinded me.

It's scary to see how much I relied on the voices of others to direct my paths. And now I see the dark silhouettes of the owners of some of these voices, and I realize they weren't for me at all. Quite the opposite, they were sent to destroy me. I see a huge monster, and his name is Religion, and I am finally brave enough to be angry with him, because he has stolen God away from me, making Him into a tame little puny judge with graying hair who raps his wooden mallet and squeaks out, "You're forever guilty."

I feel the blood rush through my veins. My feet feel light. I curse at this monster, and I slay him and feel God's power in the slashing of my sword. But all too quickly, the darkness swallows me again, and I wonder if I've really killed this monster at all, or if he'll sneak up behind me again when I least expect it.

What is most interesting to me is that though the fear washes over me in waves, there is a bravery in me I have never felt before. A willingness, a desire, a passion to fight. I'm aware of a commitment to be in the dungeon for as long as it takes. So much so that I am fighting off the hands that are reaching down for me from the light-world above. "Let us save you," they say. "Let us fix you," they call. "Let us dry your tears. Let us overwhelm you with light once again so you'll forget all of this, and it will be just a dwindling nightmare." Where were these concerned voices when I was drowning in all that light, living an empty religious life?

"Don't you dare!" I yell back. "This is not about you. I'm sorry that it makes you uncomfortable to see me this way, but you're not going to rob me of this richness. I am with God. He is here. Imagine that. In the darkness. There is no place I'd rather be. And I will come out when He says we are done, because I want to be healed this time. I want the holes in my body to be forever mended, even if there are brutal scars to show for it. When I resurface, I want to be able to contain the fullness of God within me without it leaking out all over the place. Down here, I am closer to my life to the full than I ever was soaking up sun on the beaches of pretending and performance and duty and devotion. Leave me alone. This is something I must see to."

I'm angry. I realize this. I'm tired of being fixed and tired of fixing. I've smoothed things over my whole life, wanting to assure people I was fine. And now, now I'm tired of Christian clean-up crews coming to my side every time I falter. I think I'm really angry, though, because I'm still a bit insecure. Am I really doing the right thing? Maybe they know something I don't. But then again, maybe it's necessary to be a bit angry and a bit mad to jump down into the dark rabbit hole to begin with. Maybe it takes the Mad Hatter's googly eyes, nonsensical language, and big hat to be able to deal with her royal highness, the Queen of Religion, who has been threatening to chop off my head if I don't tow the line.

What if everyone is just going through the motions, and no one is brave enough to say something? Who will say the emperor has no clothes?

I've been entertaining a lot of questions and thoughts from my dark place. I've been throwing them out to people, half to see if I would get shot at, and half to see if I could be brave enough to confess. I want to be real. I want to be vulnerable. I don't want to hide anymore. But it has been a real trying experience, because many Christians want to answer the questions for me. They want the security of the answers.

There is a misunderstanding. I just want to ask open-ended, mysterious questions that might not ever get answers. My Christian friends see them as cries for help. They are worried about me. They are concerned. One woman offered to get together regularly with me to help me better understand Jesus. At first this made me react defensively. But then I felt God speaking within me, smoothing down what I assume to be my ugly-duckling ruffled feathers. "What do you have to hide, Mandy? There is no reason to be embarrassed or ashamed. You are with Me. Relax and let them know you are with Me."

And so I do. But it's hard. Hard to say, "No, thanks." Hard to say, "I really am okay. I really don't want saved." Hard to not want to grab a hand just to alleviate their worry for me. Just as a way to say thanks for their concern. That's what a nice girl would do, right? A nice girl would come down from the cafeteria wall when offered a hand and a strong suggestion.

But this time I'm not looking for the quick spiritual fixes. I can't. I'm looking for a God who will descend to the dark places with me, throughout the entirety of my life, because I know as life ebbs and flows, there will be more descents to this dungeon. I want to be unafraid of making the trek. I want to be unafraid of facing the questions that haunt me when they arise. I want to be brave enough to sit on walls I'm not supposed to be on long enough to catch my breath and figure out for myself if I want to be there or not.

Other hands seem to reach down for me into this darkness, not to save me, but to save themselves. They aren't necessarily hands of any particular person. They are more just shadows of hands from the Christian expectations I have collected through my past. They expect me to carry on in my roles of performance.

They say to me, "Come up, won't you? We need you. We need you to support our institution. We need you to come to our event. We need you to serve in our ministry. We need you at our mom gatherings or to masquerade as the dutiful wife. We need you to make small talk. We need you to be friendly and compliant and stop asking so many questions. We need you to fall into line. To protect skeletons hidden in our closets. We need you to perform your duties as expected."

"Mend our lives," they say to me, just like in Mary Oliver's poem "The Journey."[6]

I feel like screaming out at them like the fed-up Jesus figure in the musical *Jesus Christ Superstar,* "Heal yourselves!"[7]

Instead, I yell, "Go away. I have nothing to offer you. I have nothing to give."

"How very selfish of you," they yell back down at me. And they look at each other, nodding their pure-white cloaked heads, knowing I have become what of course I would become. Hanging out in the dark side and falling off the deep end. They are suspicious of me and my character, so much so that I wonder if my skin has turned a nasty green like the Wicked Witch's in the novel *Wicked.*

"People always did like to talk, didn't they? That's why I call myself a witch now: the Wicked Witch of the West, if you want the full glory of it. As long as people are going to call you a lunatic anyway, why not get the benefit of it? It liberates you from convention," says Elphaba in *Wicked.*[8]

That is what I feel like God is doing, releasing me from convention, and I'm learning not to grab at the hands from the light or think that I owe them something. I'm learning to accept the dark and not run from it.

I'm also learning to give others the freedom to be in the light. If I don't need to be where they are all the time, they certainly don't have to be where I am all the time. It's part of a full life. Recognizing all its parts, all its shades, and giving people the grace to be in the place they are.

Robert Henri, in his book *The Art Spirit*, says it this way:

> Perhaps we delight in evening because we have had the day. Night can be painted so that it will be beautiful and true with a palette that does not drop into black but has instead a surprising richness of tone.[9]

My life is rich here in the darkness, amidst torn clothes, wet cheeks, and disheveled hair. It is a necessary part of the journey. The deeper I venture in, the brighter the stars shine, until eventually I will be lit up from within with them. Let no one steal my darkest moments, for out of them will emerge my most glorious self.

"But you don't want heavy," they say to me. "You want light. Come up here where your worries are light."

But you see, I was lied to. I was told that the yoke of being a Christ follower was easy, that the burdens were light. The burdens have not felt light. Let me tell you, every week at church, I felt as though I was being issued another task to work on. The problem is that while these tasks are all fantastic, they must also all be maintained. So a sermon series on marriage may be followed by a sermon series on sacrificing, which may be followed by a sermon series on being authentic. What I'm left with is this snowball effect of conviction that has gathered so much speed, I can hardly keep up. I'm tired of pushing it, but I know I can't stop, because that snowball is comprised of really, really important stuff.

I would be embarrassed if I had to tell you how big that snowball had gotten, but you can use your imagination. Years and years of church attendance, each week offering me a new conviction to slap onto my snowball. Why, it had gotten far bigger than the Grinch's sack of Christmas presents he stole from Whoville. I look and feel so puny beside it, and lugging it around is making me feel a little Grinch-like myself.

I was sitting in church one evening by my husband when I had this strange feeling, as if the snowball was shifting, and not in my favor. At that moment, I realized I had managed to push it up a steep incline, but I wasn't quite to the top. As I listened to my pastor talk, I became angry with him. I became angry with my church. I became angry with the people sitting on all sides of me who were drinking it all in and not questioning a thing.

I became angry that I was out of breath and just a puny, little thing, shivering with my back pressed up against an icy snowball. My toes were numb, my knees were bent, all my energy was exerted toward holding my ball of convictions in place.

I knew that there were some smaller snowballs of grace packed into my giant snowball somewhere—Sunday school lessons about Christ's forgiveness; momentary redemption found at church camp, in the words of a friend, or in the calm resolve of my parents—but I had no idea where to find them in this massive ice sculpture, and even if I did, I couldn't exactly let go of this snowball to chisel them out. I'd be crushed.

So I squatted there, cold, numb, and angry, and I realized I had two choices: I could stay here until my muscles fatigued and my determination wore thin, yelling internally at all of those Christians around me whom I hold somewhat responsible for adding to the icy proportions of this convictional mass, or I could simply do the hard task of pushing the ball two more inches to the top of the peak and then letting it roll away.

Most mountaintop experiences have done the opposite for me. I get there with my snowball feeling tired and worn out, but then I get a moment to catch my breath, and I feel my strength revitalize, and I think, *I'm ready to do this again. The downhill part is easier anyway. I just have to make sure the ball doesn't get away from me as I let its own energy do the work. I can do this.*

But this time I know it's different. I know the snowball has gotten too immense, and I am at my breaking point. I can't stay here with my butt in the seat of a church and have peace. All this place means to me is conviction, condemnation, and more snow. And I know if I stay, I'm going to get mad at God again, too, and I'm pretty sure this is not His fault.

I felt like a spy seated in the enemy camp as I sat there in church that evening. I felt numb. I wondered what my husband would think if I told him I couldn't return. I wondered what my friends would say if they didn't see me seated in the same section every Saturday night at 5:00 p.m. I wondered what Tony's staff members would say about me shirking the services at the church my husband works for. I wondered what the pastor would say to me if he knew I simply couldn't take it anymore.

I felt rebellious. I felt dishonest. I felt like a traitor, silently harboring a plan of retreat that would leave everyone dumbfounded.

And yet I felt God whispering to my soul, "Is it worth it? Is this feeling of anger and burnout you are feeling right now worth it? Is it worth hating all these people who are not the ones to blame? Is it worth it to keep pretending, keep pushing, keep feeling your heart get colder by the moment as the snowball takes its toll on your body? Who are you really hurting here? And would it be so horrible to just walk away for some time to thaw out? Some time to search for grace? Some time to remember what it feels like to not have strained muscles or numb appendages?"

Scared out of my mind and shaking from exhaustion, I heaved the ball forward with two more tiny steps up the hill. I felt it steady out on the flat plane of the peak I had been climbing for longer than I cared to remember. I let go of the snowball and came around to the other side. I had that twinge of renewed determination. I felt the adrenaline rush through my veins trying to convince me I had it in me for one more go-round. But as I watched the pastor moving on the stage, his mouth opening and closing, and as I watched the focused eyes of the audience, people hanging on his every word, I made a silent and terrified choice to place both hands on my snowball and shove it with all my might.

I was fearful that those around me might see its enormous plunge or hear the sounds of ice and snow cracking through tree branches as it plummeted. I was embarrassed that they might see little, puny me. I felt like a child sitting in that church chair, as if I were swinging my feet because they couldn't reach the ground. As if I'd have a lot of explaining to do for the mess I had just made. I felt fearful that I had no idea what to do with my body now that my convictions were gone. But there was another feeling as well. A light, airy feeling. Despite my nausea at the thought of having to tell anyone what had just happened, I had the sense that I was lifting out of my seat and flying above everyone. As if gravity had been reversed, or I was defying its laws.

A very similar vision came to me a couple of months later as I happened to be seated in my hometown church, visiting for the holidays. Finding myself in church for the first time in a while, I attempted to focus on the words being said by the pastor, but I felt myself start to float again. It felt so real and vivid that I looked around the room to see if anyone was noticing. I made eye contact with an old schoolmate up in the balcony, and I sensed he knew I wasn't grounded and that he longed to be floating too. I smiled despite myself, thinking of offering a hand to him so that he could float above the heads of the focused churchgoers as well. I replayed the song "Defying Gravity" from the musical *Wicked* in my mind, the words feeling all too appropriate: "I'm defying gravity / And you can't pull me down!"[10]

I giggled internally at the thought of distracting the congregation with my flight to the ceiling. People reaching to grab an arm or a leg to get me back down and in my place. Many of these people had watched me grow up. It was risky to step out of a mold your hometown has seen you fit best in.

This didn't feel like an elitist sort of floating, although I'm sure it could be interpreted as such. Rather, the floating was occurring because my soul was lighter than air, and there was nothing left to keep me grounded. I realized this is what it feels like to not have complete control of my life and yet be okay with that. To laugh like the old man in *Mary Poppins* who floats to the ceiling despite himself.

Oops, I've gone too far, the laws of gravity have been reversed, and I'm free.

While I was in my hometown church, another very interesting thing happened. At the beginning of the service, shortly after an opening song, we had some time to meet and greet other church attenders. In my parents' church, this didn't mean the typical turn around and shake hands with one or two people in the pews behind you and then face forward and shake hands with one or two people in front of you. On the contrary, in their church it meant leaving your pew and walking clear across the other side of the sanctuary to hug a friend. I stayed put and silently wished the band would resume its music.

Suddenly, out of the corner of my eye, I saw my junior high volleyball coach approaching our pew. She said hi to my mom, who hadn't wandered far away yet, and then she came and shook hands with me. She looked the same—blonde hair, tan, fit, pretty—but her eyes seemed distant, as though she were meeting someone for the first time.

"Hey! How are you?" I asked warmly.

She tilted her head and furled her brow a bit in confusion. She kept shaking my hand, gripping it tightly and leaning in a bit closer, as if she were leaning in to peer into my brain to see what sort of memories I had with her. I recognized she had no idea who I was.

"Have we met before?" she asked, confirming my assumption.

"I'm Mandy. I played volleyball on your team in junior high." I said it slowly, giving her time to make the connection.

"Oh," she said, and then, "OH!" she screamed. She looked back and forth between me and my mom, realizing exactly who I was. Then she did the unexpected. She grabbed my face in her hands, pushed back my bangs, leaned in even closer, and said, "Mandy! Of course it's you."

She pulled me in close to hug me, and then she grabbed my hands and leaned back to take me all in.

"Wow, you look beautiful," she said. "You look so different. I completely didn't recognize you. Maybe it's the bangs?"

I wanted to tell her it's more than the bangs. I'm an entirely different person. I blinked a bit shyly and looked to my mom and then to Tony to see if they were noticing this whole conversation. They were. Then I looked back at my childhood coach and said, "Thank you. You look great yourself."

By now church members were beginning to trickle back into their seats, so she said, "It's so good to see you." We hugged again, and she shook her head with a sort of disbelief as she walked back across the room to her pew.

I felt a lightness in my spirit after that interaction. I felt pleased. I *have* changed. I'm not who I once was. My own coach didn't recognize me. I have broken out of that scared, bruised Mandy cocoon, and my wings are unfolding on either side of me, displaying a beauty I'm not familiar with, or altogether comfortable with. But it's me. It's me. It's finally me!

I have changed.

I am changing.

And my wingspan no longer fits in the cocoon.

The Divine is inviting me outside of myself to become something I had once only hoped for. And here I have this fantastic concrete story to remember my progress whenever I have my doubts. I am not who I once was. I'm free.

I think a lot about those intimate church moments with God. How symbolic it was that He would speak to my heart inside the church at the very same time the pastor was speaking for Him. I think about how hard it has been to hear His voice in my own thoughts when there are so many other voices telling me what to believe and what actions need to be taken. I think about how real that moment was and how delightfully magical. A change, an invitation, a permission, a risk.

The burden really is light; the yoke really is easy. I'm the one who often makes it too hard, pushing on the icy sides of a snowball I assume everyone expects me to care for. Maybe I hadn't been lied to after all, but it took an enormous snowball fight to wake me up and thaw me out. It took a painful moment of popping antigravity pills in what felt like the enemy's camp for me to gain this new perspective.

Maybe we're meant to fly along that narrow road instead of walk, a little less burdened by the journey, a little less angry about having to make it.

Chapter Nine

Toast

A couple of days ago, I had a cup of warm tea with my breakfast. The container said it was a "Tea for Wisdom." As I stood in the kitchen waiting for the teakettle to whistle, my belly pressed up against the counter, I read the rest of the tea packaging and found this insightful quote:

> I say you can trace the whole mess on this planet
> to the fact that we lose ourselves in ideas for living
> while life awaits us to inhabit it.

I took it as a delightful message meant personally for me, but as delightful as it was, it equally required some wrestling.

I do like ideas. I do like to sit and journal and read and think, to philosophize and dream, to make lists and try to improve myself and my life. Perhaps I enjoy it more than the actual living out of my life. It's certainly less scary, less interrupted, less messy.

Internally anything is possible. I can wander to my heart's content. I can feel invincible. I can dream impressive dreams, leading myself out of dark and into light. But eventually there comes the necessary rubbing of shoulders with real live people who may not go along peaceably with my life's plan of attack.

Ideas are unencumbered by things unforeseen. As well thought out as they may be, when it's time to make the transition from thinking to active living, things never go as prettily as planned.

There is this other thing about ideas: sometimes the constant running of my brain just plain gives me a headache. I set out so passionately to solve some problem or answer some question in my life, but many times I think myself in circles, arriving back where I started and wondering if that was time well spent or well wasted.

There are some moments when I have to force myself to give up the thinking so I don't make myself mad. Some questions just can't be answered. In fact, I've been wondering lately, after soaking up my tea wisdom, if it isn't better to let life's unfolding answer the questions naturally instead of missing out on life to force some sort of unnatural answer. Rainer Maria Rilke speaks to this in his *Letters to a Young Poet:*

> Be patient toward all that is unsolved in your heart
> and try to love the questions themselves, like locked
> rooms and like books that are written in a very for-
> eign tongue. Do not now seek the answers, which
> cannot be given you because you would not be able
> to live them. And the point is, to live everything.
> Live the questions now. Perhaps you will then grad-
> ually, without noticing it, live along some distant
> day into the answer.[1]

I have quite a life to inhabit right now. There is no shortage of activity, what with four little kiddios ages seven and under, and my husband and I both highly driven. Some days it feels as though we jump to our feet in the morning and hold our breath until we jump back off them at night, landing in our beds soundly.

I'm learning to make time for myself amidst this bustle, because no one freely offers it up for me. In my quiet time to myself, I sit and journal about life as it could be, the new me I'd like to step into, the fearful person I have been for far too long. This time is precious, priceless, and necessary to me, but I'm a bit concerned on the days that I think the answer is to just freeze myself in my perfect alone moments. To think life is happening solely here where everything makes sense on paper, and I'm fully loving myself, because there is no one to call my ideas into question.

What I presume of God in these moments is beautiful and intimate, and I hear Him clearly. Much more clearly than I do on a day when my kids are fighting that "He keeps taking my truck" and "She keeps cheating in the game" and complaining, "Why do we have to have rice and beans for supper when we hate rice and beans?" All the while the beans are burning on the stove, and my husband is ready to be picked up with the one car we manage to share.

I'm trying to get my ideas to bleed into my reality. Sometimes I manage to do so, if the stars are aligned and I'm holding my breath just right and the weather is just so and the toddler is napping. But most days I feel as though I am one person on paper and another entirely different person in the flesh.

The stark reality of this hit me about a month ago when one of my dearest friends, Teresa, invited me and my kids to spend the night for a slumber party. I'll speak more about Teresa in later chapters, because she plays a key character in my story, but for now I must just relay the slumber-party incident.

The reason this overnighter at Teresa's home was such an interesting dynamic was because I typically meet with her one-on-one over dinner or coffee while my kids are home with their dad. Our conversations are magical and inspiring. Time flies by when we're together, and I leave her presence with a renewed confidence in myself and my ability to hear from and be loved on by God. I leave her with a passion to jump back into life as I know it. I expected that this slumber party, though a little more chaotic, would deliver the same sort of empowered feelings. I was wrong.

It wasn't that my children were horribly misbehaved; it's just that there are four of them, and they were in a new environment, and their curiosity was at an all-time high. I was instantly on edge. What should I let them touch and what shouldn't I? The television was on, and it was sucking their ability to be polite. They were so zoned, they couldn't answer questions about what they wanted to eat. They couldn't hear me say, "It's time to get your pajamas on," and they certainly were far too wired to think about going to sleep when bedtime rolled around. My toddler kept climbing out of his bed, and the room they were sharing with Teresa's toddler granddaughter was utter mayhem.

I just wanted to sit and talk and conjure up that same magical spirit that usually permeates my times with Teresa. My idea of a slumber party looked vastly different. My kids were with me, and I would have to wear my parenting hat, a hat that is still far too big for my head and sits rather sloppily over my ears, threatening at any moment to fall down completely and plunge me into darkness. Unfortunately it is also a hat I wear more to please others. I haven't settled into Mandy as the Mother. In fact, Mandy as the Mother is part of the reason I have to write this book to begin with, because this hat has made me lose my real identity almost entirely.

I have never been so glaringly aware of the differences in me as I was that night at the slumber party. I was a bit embarrassed for Teresa to see me as a mom who has no idea how to enjoy myself when I feel I must make my children perform at their best. Heaped upon my shoulders, which are working so hard to be free of a heavy yoke, is this unexplored pressure to create perfect children with good manners who obey the rules.

Why? Why? Why?

Because if I don't, then I have failed as a parent and as a home-school mom and as a person. (Let's not mention at this point that I am also the messy woman who is trying so desperately to free myself from the need to be perfect, tow the line, obey the rules. Let's not mention that it seems a bit ludicrous that I would find it so necessary to be teaching my children what I am trying to unteach myself.)

I went into that evening with an idea in my head, and each unpredictable moment left me uneasy with the reality of how out of control this all felt. I wanted to go home. I wanted to go home where I could tuck my kids into bed when 8:30 p.m. came around, and where I would know that for the most part, they would stay where tucked, and I could have some time to myself. I wanted to be where the rhythms were safe and routine, so I didn't have to deal with this part of me that is far more messy than I look on paper, confined to my idea world.

That night, when I finally did crawl into bed, I noticed that my blankets were folded back for me, a loving expression I wasn't prepared to meet. As I situated myself among the sweet-smelling, cozy sheets, I began to cry. I cried for how lousy a mom I felt I was and for how high-strung I seemed to be. I cried for how much further I had to go to actually unearth the Mandy who had gotten buried by a life of performance and, most recently, by a duty to my role of wife and mom. I cried for how vulnerable and naked and ugly I had felt in front of Teresa, simply because I couldn't let this night be different from all my other one-on-one encounters with her.

I cried for expectations I could never meet, and for those I felt were being stripped out of my hands despite every effort on my part to hide behind them. I cried at the feminine unconditional love that had folded back my blankets despite how grumpy and gloomy and depressed I had acted. I cried as I felt God revealing a more feminine side to the Divine than I had ever seen, a side that said, "You are loved for you, not for how well you perform or how good you are at relaxing and having fun."

I felt my insides screaming.

I'm not laid back.

I'm not a free spirit.

I never will be.

I'm not good at this word messy *You're asking me to live out. I don't want a messy life anymore. I hate how this all looked and felt tonight. I'm humiliated, and I don't know how to change it. I didn't even manage to brush my own teeth! I was too busy taking care of everyone else.*

When this parenting hat is on, I forget about the me *You are telling me I am. Perhaps I can't hear You because it's covering my ears.*

I feel so clumsy and frumpy.

I do not feel like an artist.

This is far less romantic than I expected.

Right before I fell asleep, I realized how intensely I was trying to do this on my own. I wanted to stop having people stare at me and critique me. To stop feeling like the center-ring circus attraction. I wanted to be able to stop staring at and critiquing myself.

As I flailed, God was a warm feminine presence holding me, loosely, gently. Telling me, *Mandy, I love you right now. Not just in our times on paper, not just in your idea world, but right now, in your mess.*

I ran out of energy for my tantrum, and despite myself, I settled into a warm bed with covers that had been lovingly pulled back just for me. I succumbed to the comfort and love I was searching for.

Now, a month later, I recall those thoughts in the light of this tea wisdom, and I think, *Where does this bring me? How do I fully inhabit the life I am actually living? How do I become more than my ideas?*

I must first be fully known as who I am in order to ever be fully known as who I long to be.

Am I capable of embracing a life that unfolds so uncontrollably, so sporadically, and in such a messy fashion? Am I capable of letting ideas bend and morph until they become something quite different entirely? Am I capable of living at an arm's length from busyness and performance and rigid routine and people pleasing?

Last night was a tough night for me. My four-year-old was up five times during the night. Almost every hour on the hour, I would awake to his loud and confused cries. I never did figure out what exactly his problem was. Was it his usual growing pains intensified? Was it nightmares? He did mention, in one incoherent slur, that there were monsters after him. Was it his finger? We had discovered just yesterday that it was bruised and swollen and red with pain. I don't know, because he wouldn't ever tell me. I could never get a clear answer from him, just loud cries.

The first time he woke up was at midnight. Having just pondered this tea wisdom before going to bed, it was fresh on my mind. I had also just watched the movie *Shirley Valentine*, an amusing look at one woman's search for her identity through the muddled roles of wife and mom. I'd finished the movie with a glowing sense of "There is still time to do this right. I still have time to live the life I'm wanting to live." Those thoughts were still ringing in my ears.

As my son laid down beside me in my bed this first time, by far his most coherent time, he mentioned that his belly hurt. I asked my typical question, "Like you're going to throw up?"

And he said, "No, like I'm hungry."

I realized instantly that this was an opportunity. I went through an entire inner dialogue before I got up the guts to take action.

I could go make him some toast. We could eat it in the kitchen with some warm milk. It would be our little midnight date.

You're getting up early tomorrow. Your alarm is set for 5:00 a.m. You need to get up early because you have a lot to do. You have to exercise because you didn't yesterday. And you have to

write because you haven't in a few days. And you'll need that alone time to get your head on straight for a new week of being a mom to four little needy souls. Plus it's laundry day.

Remember that scene in the book A Wrinkle in Time,[2] where the mom and Charles Wallace and Meg all drink warm drinks together in the kitchen during a bad storm in the middle of the night? I've always found it so endearing. I've always wanted a life like that.

You know if you do this once, he's going to think you'll do it every night. Do you want to be up every night making toast for a four-year-old when you should be sleeping? Think about yourself. You've got to look out for yourself.

I am thinking about myself and how I've always wanted to be the person who would get up and have a piece of pie in the kitchen at four in the morning when the mood strikes me. I don't have pie, and it's not 4:00 a.m., but this is as good a start as any.

This is ludicrous. You're not even making sense. That's not the kind of life you want. You know how angsty you get when you haven't exercised or written. I'm trying to protect you here. Put the boy back in his own bed. Or at the very most, let yourself fall asleep with him beside you. He's quiet again.

I remember Teresa talking one time about when her kids were little, sometimes they'd look at the stars at 3:00 a.m. I remember how invigorating it felt to realize that I could do the very same thing. That I'm not tied down to any sort of schedule. That literally I have the whole week, minus two or three commitments, to do whatever I want. I have the world at my fingertips, with all the freedom a girl could desire, and I'm worried about whether or not I'll have the energy to do laundry? Is this what my life has come to?

Oh, don't go getting all romantic. Real life must be lived, too, you know. This isn't some fairy tale you get to flit around in. Those clothes aren't going to wash themselves, nor will your muscles strengthen themselves or your book write itself. You're going to be tired. Don't you feel it swallowing you up already, and you know if you get tired, you get angry. And if you get angry, you start yelling at your kids. And don't you already have enough guilt about yelling at your kids?

I could take a nap. At any given moment tomorrow, I could take a nap. I have the freedom to do that. And I have the freedom to make my son toast and warm milk at midnight.

And with that, I ended the conversation with myself, put my son's hand in mine, and said, "Come on, buddy. Come with me."

He didn't want to sit at the kitchen table, because he was too cold and too tired. I realized he'd never had warm milk, and though it worked for Charles Wallace and Meg, I wasn't sure if it would work for him, so I poured him his own little glass of cold milk. As I waited for the bread to toast, I covered him up on the couch with an afghan from his grandma. I noticed how skinny his body was, how little he still was. I realized there was still plenty of time. Life hadn't ended and left me regretful. I still had time. The toast popped up, and he realized what I was doing. I was making him a treat. A midnight snack. Something I had never done for him. He smiled warmly, looking out at me from his squinted eyes. I smiled back, warmly, unforced.

I buttered his toast and pulled a little end table up by his head for his milk and toast to rest on. I told him to take his time and to let me know when he was ready to go back to bed. I laid down on the other couch, covered myself with another grandma afghan, and closed my eyes.

You'll never have the patience or energy to do this again, the voice inside my head hissed at me.

I don't have to. I just had to say yes to this moment. I just had to make one solitary choice for right now. I just had to have enough patience and energy for tonight. And you know what? I did

Chapter Ten

So?

Once upon a time there was a little girl who liked to please her dad. That little girl grew up into a twenty-one-year-old girl who still liked to please her dad, but who fell in love, got married, and moved three hours away, at which point she quickly fell into the role of the not-so-little girl who liked to please her husband. She wouldn't notice the repercussions of this for ten years, and by then, the behavior would be entirely habitual (or addictive) and nearly impossible to change.

I wrote a novel last November for National Novel Writing Month. I think I needed to write it to clue in to the fact that I wasn't living the life I wanted to live. My main character, Elise, was a woman who was practically forced into doing a lot of soul searching, and she soon realized she was living a life that fit in well with what her husband wanted.

It wasn't as if he'd ever verbally communicated his requests to her. That would have been far too obvious. Instead, over time, there had been this unspoken law of the land. She had learned his nonverbals, memorized his reactions, witnessed his preferences, and made her own assumptions, and she, being so inclined to avoid conflict and play nice, had learned to take all of those things into consideration before making any personal decisions. She had learned to edit her life to not only please him but to also include him as much as possible. She thought, as his wife, she should strive to always include him.

In one section of the novel, Elise went into an inner monologue, anxiously realizing, *My schedule is dependent upon his willingness to take part. My fun is dependent upon his compliance.* She felt trapped into living a life she no longer wanted to live. What would happen if she started exerting her "independence"? Would her husband notice? Would he be bothered by it?

A few months after writing the novel, I was gripped in my own life by this fear of how my life would turn out if I kept waiting to be happy. I wondered what I was waiting for. Was I waiting for my husband to participate in all the fun things I would like to do or try? Was I waiting for my husband's approval to behave a certain way? Was I waiting for my kids to be the perfect age so they don't require so much of me? Was I waiting for permission from my church or from friends or from my own parents? What was holding me back from being happy?

I realized that parts of my dreams included this perfect image of a family who did fun things together, who laughed together, who went on adventures together. I had managed to concoct a delightful future for myself that demanded everyone's participation and enjoyment. My husband would have to play out this role dutifully; my kids would have to all fall into line to carry out their parts. There was this strange assumption on my part, seeing how I am the wife and the mom and the one who feels as if I orchestrate this big symphony called family life, that I needed to dream dreams big enough for us all. That my vision of happiness had to include everyone. No wonder I felt trapped, lugging along all their weight to live out a vision of happiness I didn't even clearly see myself, let alone had never communicated to them.

I wrote this in my journal last spring: "I feel like all I'm doing is getting mad at Tony, because I'm not living the life *I* want to be. Like I'm casting blame. I'm wishing for God knows what and feeling empty that I'm not getting it." Meanwhile I was dutifully keeping house and making meals, being everyone's conscience, and enforcing disciplines as if I were a robot doing what I'd been programmed to do. I noticed in my journal from last spring that I had started a dream list of things I wanted to do with Tony. It was scratched out in messy black ink, and a new list was started on the next page titled, "Dreams that Don't Depend on Anyone but God and Me."

It's all starting to make sense to me now, the journey I have been on. Writing the novel and journaling about independent dreams have contributed to the life I am living right now, the place of near burnout. The place of shaking my head, coming out of my daze, and wondering how I've managed to live in such a limited fashion. The novel was a safe place to say hard things, because it wasn't me saying them. It was a character in a novel. She gave me the confidence to start asking those questions in my own life, even if just on paper in my private journal, and that has given me the confidence to ask them now, out loud to myself in this book.

Mandy, why are you living a life that will please Tony and please your kids and please your parents and please your friends and please your church? And why especially would you keep on living this life if you aren't happy and you feel the Divine inviting you into something much more exciting?

Why are you living a life that is dependent on everyone else's happiness but yours? And what makes you think that taking care of yourself for a change is going to make their lives fall apart? Is it possible that they don't need you to arrange for their happiness quite like you've assumed? Is it possible that it isn't selfish to consider your own needs sprinkled in among your other responsibilities?

What is it you want that you're not getting? Are you scared to know the answer? Are you scared because there is no answer? Are you scared because you've lost yourself so completely in performing for others that you've forgotten entirely what it is you're even passionate about?

Are you scared to break the rules you yourself created over the years, the rules based on assumptions, hurt feelings, and not wanting to make waves?

Tony once shared with me a striking visual image, and it keeps haunting me. There is, in my case, a woman, standing in a box. She feels suffocated and trapped, so much so that her breathing is labored and her temples feel as if the pressure pushing in on them is too much to bear. She can't stretch out her arms fully because the box is too small. Her body aches. She feels tiny and helpless. Suddenly her eyes manage to pan away from her own toes for a split second, and she sees that outside the painted whites lines of this box is a field. She's standing in a big open field that stretches out as far as her eyes can see. She slowly turns around in a circle to take it all in. In every direction there are acres of land to be seen; up above her the sky opens up into an ever-expanding palette of blue.

She looks back down at her box. She notices for the first time that the box is literally just painted grass. She is standing in one tiny section of that enormous field, and the only thing holding her in isn't walls, or bars, but a tiny square painted around her feet. Her heartbeat races. Is it true? Is it possible? Could she really just lift one foot and step outside the square and be free? Why, it's impossible! If it were true, why had she never noticed it before? The strangest thing is, she is terrified of lifting her foot.

It reminds me a bit of having knee surgery as a teenager. I distinctly remember the first time I tried to take a shower. There I was, all naked, feeling vulnerable. My leg was exposed and smelling horrible. It was black and blue and yellow. It looked sickly, too skinny, my muscles atrophied from lack of use. The bottom of the shower was raised only about three inches, but you would have thought it was as tall as I was. I willed my leg to lift that high but could barely raise my toes off the ground. I lowered myself down gingerly onto the bathroom tile floor and cried. How could this be so hard? Would I ever be able to do it?

The woman in the visual plops down on the earth, careful to keep her body inside the white painted box on the grass. She notices she is shaking. She begins to cry. How could this be so hard? Would she ever be able to do it?

I'm beginning to make choices in my life that aren't my typical choices. Choices I've wanted to make but haven't for fear of either disturbing the peace or getting made fun of. They are simple choices, but when people are used to you behaving a certain way, even the simplest of choices can raise eyebrows.

I've started incorporating some alone time for me as I need it. This often looks like a midafternoon nap. I explained to my kids that I need to have some time alone to regroup. That one mom taking care of four kiddios can get tiresome, and I have to have some rest. To say I'm giddy to have this time is an understatement. I know throughout my day, no matter how many fights I've had to break up or how many messes I've had to clean up, I have this little pocket of my own time to look forward to. I give my kiddios options for how they can self-entertain, then I take a book and my journal and sometimes a snack; and I head to the solitude of my room. I am overjoyed to get to be by myself behind a closed door.

I've created a sacred place on my nightstand, a personal little altar of sorts. There is a Mother Mary candle and a set of nesting dolls that remind me of the feminine nature of God. There is an inspiration board where I pin up images or words that move me. There are chocolate treats in my top drawer—that is, if I haven't consumed them all already. There is a box full of little treasures I've been given, like rocks and crystals and marbles and such. There are books of poetry for when I need to slow down and be reminded of the mystery and beauty around me. It's all created for me to feel loved and valued and appreciated. Contrary to what I used to believe, I don't need to wait for someone else to do this for me.

I have gotten quite good at redirecting wandering kiddios who open my door during my rest time. Sometimes there is a lot of huffing and puffing that I won't wait on them hand and foot. I must remind them, sometimes more gently than others, "Now is not the time to ask me to play Uno with you or to read a book to you or to get you a snack or to make your brother stop looking at you. We've had all morning together. Now is the time for you to find something to entertain yourself."

Do you know how hard it is to carve out this time for myself and not feel like a lousy mom because of it? Especially when my children look at me all dejected, heads drooping, eyes watery. Or when they get angry and slam my door and scream, "Fine! You never play with me anymore." They expect me to behave the same way I have always behaved, but I'm just not that person anymore. I'm the person who carves out my own little moments to help me savor life to the full. It's not flawless, but it helps.

"Do I have any clean underwear?" Tony yells from upstairs. This used to send me into a tailspin. *Oh great, I haven't put his laundry away. He is going to have to walk downstairs to get it. He's going to be so annoyed. I better stop writing and take it up to him.* Or I would get defensive and think, *Does that man ever do anything for himself?*

The new me is daring to look at things a different way. Perhaps this is the way of the narrow path. This isn't something to get defensive about. The man isn't calling into question my character; he's simply asking for a pair of underwear. Nor is this something to interrupt my work for. He may be irritated, but I can't do everything. Some weeks the clean clothes just don't get put away. At least they got washed. So the new me is trying to respond simply with, "Yes, you do. It's down here in a laundry basket on the dryer."

The new me knows it can be just that simple. Someone asks a question. I give an answer. It may not be the answer they like, but it is the reality for the moment, and I don't need to apologize or overexplain or react defensively for that reality. I have done the best I can.

This has been happening in other little ways as well.

I call and cancel an engagement I said I would attend. I'm learning to not be scared of adjusting my commitments.

I arrive later at a place than I was supposed to, but I know I did my best.

I keep my phone on silent so I don't have to be bothered when I'm doing something with my kids.

I don't always answer emails or Facebook messages. I can't get to everything. Not everything is an emergency.

I plan time away for my own renewal. I tell Tony when I'm feeling burned-out. I don't let things fester. I say what I feel I need to say.

I say no to opportunities I don't have the resources for, and no to commitments that don't interest me. I can't make it to that baby shower. I can't do that graphic-design piece for you. I can't buy the things you're selling me.

I say yes to things I do want to do, even if it means I have to do them all by myself. I make my desires known. I want to stay at the bike race. I would like to get my nose pierced. I want to go on a date. I want to get my hair cut. I want to see this movie.

I remember telling Tony I wanted to see the movie *The King's Speech*, and that I was planning on going one evening if he'd be up for watching the kids.

"Of course you can go," he told me. "Who are you going to see it with?" he asked.

"By myself."

"Well, you can do that if that's what you want, but I would really love to go see it with you if you want company and we can find a babysitter."

We ended up seeing the movie together, an impromptu date, and the movie spoke to him as much as it did me. It worked out for both of us.

I'm learning to take ownership for my choices. I want to do things because I really have a desire to do them, not because it would please someone. If what I want to do doesn't pan out, I try not to freak out. I tell myself the no is not forever. The no is just for right now. Maybe there are better things for me in the present.

I learned about detachment from a book called *Addiction and Grace*. I learned that in our culture, we have come to define that word negatively, when in fact its original meaning was very healthy. Attachment nails our desire to specific objects and creates addiction. Detachment is a liberation of those desires.[1]

I realized that my desire for meaning and love and approval has been attached to achieving and performing and succeeding, and when I feel I'm failing at doing these things, I become depressed. I am awakening, at this time in my life, to a need for detachment. To detach myself from all the people I think I'm performing for. To be detached is to not care what another person thinks of me, because my value isn't nailed to that person's approval of my performance. To be detached is to run around in a field when once I had been trapped in a painted white square.

The night we returned from *The King's Speech*, I had a hard conversation with Tony. I kept starting the conversation in my mind, trying to get the words right. I was nervous. I wanted to communicate how hard it was as a woman to have the confidence to be vulnerable with my artistic voice. How could I write about my own spiritual questions and discoveries all the while knowing that he is a pastor? Would I make him look bad? Would he disagree with my theology?

How do I create passionately as a woman without feeling like I'm just being silly or too emotional or dramatic? I feel like many times I'm held back by my fear of what he will think of me. But how do I communicate that without making him feel bad?

I need to have the freedom to be myself, to be allowed to be something other than Tony's wife, bowing in submission to all the rules and commandments I've somehow assumed he wants me to follow. I ease into the conversation, using *The King's Speech* as a natural lead-in.

"I think it's easier for a man to assert himself and say what he needs to say than it is for a woman. I'm processing a lot of hard stuff right now that I need to get out on paper. Like how I think God isn't the patriarch I've always known Him to be. That His character has feminine *and* masculine qualities." I pause, waiting to see Tony's reaction. He is listening.

"It's been really big for me lately to have some males respond positively to the content on my blog. To have them encourage me and even agree with what I'm processing. It makes me feel like I'm not crazy. That maybe God really is teaching me things, and maybe He could really use my feminine voice."

"I'm glad," he responds. He doesn't have a lot of words for me, and I have plenty for him. I realize, as I'm getting all this out, that this is the first time I've given him a glimpse into what I've been processing. He knows I'm struggling with my faith. He knows I'm not in church. He knows I'm not reading my Bible, save for Galatians. He knows I'm discovering God in new, rich ways. But he doesn't know the intimate issues I've been grappling with. I've tried to save my words for Teresa. I've tried to save my thought processes for my journal, for this book, for God. I'm in such a fragile place, I don't want to get trampled on, or worse yet, written off.

"I'm just scared," I said to him, "that if I live the way or write the way I feel like God is revealing to me, you'll just roll your eyes at me."

"I might," he said matter-of-factly. "But so what?"

Though my eyes started to well up with tears at his brutal honesty and at the thought of him rolling his eyes at my attempt to live out my life passionately, honestly, and in the best messy way I know how, there was a part of me inside that came alive. A part of me that put my chin up and said in a healthy, detached voice of agreement, "Yeah, so what?!"

"Mandy, I trust God with you. I don't need to be in control of you. I'm not worried about you. I believe everything you're going through is just making you into a stronger, more beautiful woman. And I do believe you're an artist and that God is going to use you and your words."

I'm relieved to hear that. I'm relieved that he is so calm about my adventures and discoveries and exploration with the Divine. I'm relieved that he isn't expecting me to be a trophy wife. I am relieved that we don't have to agree on everything to still be married. I'm also relieved that I am strong enough for his "So what?"

It is the *So what?!* that keeps me writing this morning, that keeps me writing most mornings when all I want to do is climb back under the covers and hide. It is the *So what?!* that keeps me asking questions that are too big for me to answer. It is the *So what?!* that propels me forward when I'm shaking in a field of tears, having withdrawals as I detox from performing, all the while wondering why I'm so messed up.

It is the *So what?!* that helps me through the dark places when everyone is telling me to just come back out where it is safe and live off of the script that has been prewritten for me. It is the *So what?!* that gives me the courage to continue searching for other women, like myself, who have lost themselves and then found themselves again. We are a minority, but our voices together are loud, and they must be heard if we are to encourage one another to truly go after the life to the full that has been promised to us.

One early morning, I was sitting, typing at my computer, working on edits for this book, when Tony came downstairs.

"I had a horrible dream," he said, rubbing his eyes as if he were trying to make sure he was truly awake. "It was so real. You were leaving with this other man. I couldn't see what he looked like clearly. I didn't recognize him, but it was so lifelike and painful." He paused. "And I woke up too soon. I didn't even get to make it to the part of the dream where I throw the guy against the wall," he said, smiling.

Immediately I thought, *This is all your fault, Mandy. This quest to find yourself is leaving everybody a bit crazed. Maybe it's time to tame it down or knock it off altogether. What's the use? Just go back to being nice Mandy who keeps everyone's world peaceful.*

But another thought came to me. *Yes, Mandy, you are changing. Yes, you are different. No, you are not the same woman he married, but he isn't the same man either.*

I turned to look at him. "I'm not going anywhere. You can't get rid of me that easily. I don't have to run away from my life to find a new, fuller one. I'm just in the process of opening my eyes to the one I already have."

A little later in the morning, we discussed who would have the car for the day. Tony usually commutes to work by bike, but he had errands he needed to run, so he needed the car.

"I'm just still a bit tentative after that dream to push for something I want. I don't want to upset you," he said, laughing and pulling me in close for a hug.

"I appreciate your concern for me, but I would let you know if I needed the car. I'm getting better at knowing and saying what I need."

As he walked toward the garage door to leave, I felt the urge to share something that had been racing through my mind. I realized he might laugh at me and my eccentric ways of seeing signs in everything, but *so what?!*, right? I had to risk it.

"Hey, Tony."

He turned to look at me, his hand on the door. "Yeah?"

"I think you were the man in the dream that I ran away with. I think you just didn't recognize yourself because you've changed so much. We both have."

He didn't laugh. On the contrary, he actually looked as if he was contemplating my dream interpretation. Then he looked straight into my eyes, intensely, warmly, and said, "You know, you may be right."

Chapter Eleven

Mystery

We wake, if we ever wake at all, to mystery.

—Annie Dillard, *Pilgrim at Tinker Creek*

I decided last night that I have no business writing a book. I've read a few of them in my day, and it seems that the formula goes like this: live life, figure something out, write about it. Memoir-type writing such as what I am doing isn't written in the weeds. It's written after you've made it through them and are able to see the whole picture. It's written with a hindsight that has far greater perspective. I realized this last night as Teresa encouraged me to write down the questions of my heart.

"But there are so many of them," I told her via text message. "Far too many to be writing a book as if I have answers."

She assured me, "This is the perfect time to be writing a book. It's a how-to in the midst; a learn-as-you-go kind of writing."

It certainly is that. This kind of writing is messy.

So this morning I turn up my haunting instrumental Celtic music in my headphones, and I sit down, once again, to honor this commitment to writing. I think about my friend who teases me about liking bagpipes a little too much. I think about how foolish it appears to be obsessed with something, anything. Then I think about how artists have to obsess over something in order to create. It's par for the course. I have to do what I have to do.

I feel a bit like Jeremiah in the Bible. A prophet who was laughed at, ignored, ridiculed. A prophet who came across as a bit obsessed. I wonder if prophets and artists are made from the same materials. I try on the name *Prophetess* for the fun of it. I find it rather looming, but also entirely enchanting.

I ask my friend Carlos if he thinks artists are prophets. He says he does. He's superexcited because he says he just received that same sort of revelation when he was at a speaking event last week. I'm relieved to hear that. I'm relieved whenever I don't feel so alone. Is God speaking the same words to His artists as He is to His prophets?

If we are prophets, things are surely going to get messy. And I'm nervous because I may not interpret or translate or transcribe the words just right. What if I misunderstand the Muse?

This writing is risky, but it is as Teresa called it. It's "learn as you go." My agent tells me people connect with honesty. I have that much going for me. If nothing else, I can be raw and honest. So I sit down this morning, and I honor this commitment to myself, this commitment to the Divine, because He always seems to meet me here, in the spaces between the words, and He soothes the searching and seeking and striving.

He soothes the ache and confusion and reminds me that this haunting feeling and these questions are just my soul longing to connect to Him. And He is here. Not containably, as I think I want, but intimately, knowing me on a level I can hardly know myself. Not formulaically so that I can figure Him out once and for all, but mysteriously so that my heart and soul won't grow bored or calloused or sleepy. Not logically so that I can easily explain and prove the intensity and beauty of Him to another, but resolutely so that I am sure internally of my spiritual interactions with Him and brave enough to be changed externally.

I have come to the conclusion—if one can make conclusions at only thirty-two years of age—that the most important aspect of faith and spirituality is mystery. If we could embrace mystery, we might be able to embrace God Himself, at least momentarily, before He flits around the corner inviting us to chase Him in another adventure. Of course, mystery is also the very thing we think we want the least. Give me answers, solutions, clarity. Don't make me wrestle or question or wonder. Let me know what to expect; give me the game plan, the rules, the agenda, so I can prepare, so I can maintain proper control. Don't surprise me, interrupt me, or ask me to change my assumptions. Let me just have it all figured out.

I was telling Teresa last night that something still felt as if it was missing in this journey I'm on to find myself. As I talked through that a bit more with her, I explained I felt a disconnect between my alone times and my times with others, much like what I felt that night at her home when I took my kids there for a slumber party.

It seems I cannot properly carry the revelations in a container that can withstand the impact of the "real world." Just as I go to open up and share the real me and the real God with those I love, the container turns into mist in my hands, leaving me feeling empty and ashamed, as if I made up all those intimate words God and I had exchanged. As if the beauty I had experienced in His presence isn't transferrable in the exchange rate of normal life. There is no currency to properly monetize it.

I believe this, too, is part of the mystery. It's why the moments we feel we really see the Divine or understand the Divine or cleave to the Divine make such an impact on us, because we know they are momentary. In our limited humanity, we want to be able to hold Him in our palms and say, "This is it. I've got You. The secret to all happiness. Come everyone and look." But I suppose if we were able to hold God in our palms, we would eventually become disenchanted with something so finite.

"God becomes and God unbecomes," Meister Eckhart, German mystic theologian, once said. I am taken by the mystics because they managed to see God in everything. I love Meister Eckhart's idea that we learn God, we encounter Him, we are given an image to build an understanding of His deity on, and just as quickly, He changes forms, and we unlearn Him in that old way so that we can relearn Him in a new way. In this sense, if we can keep up with His movement, our faith will never have the opportunity to become dry or brittle.

John O'Donohue, in an interview with Krista Tippett, translates Eckhart's statement in his own words by saying, "God is only our name for it, and the closer we get to it, the more it ceases to be God. So then you are on a real safari with the wildness and danger and otherness of God.... And I think when you begin to get a sense of the depth that is there[,] then your whole heart wakens up."[1]

The hard part is trusting in a God who loves us better than we can love ourselves, but whom we can't seem to get to the bottom of. We think in order to love Him, we must know Him fully in a way that is concrete.

True love is never concrete. It is always unfolding. It's why we awake to a new day and can think, *I love my husband more today than I did yesterday,* or, *My heart could burst for my kids. I love them even more today than the day they were born.* It is also why our hearts jump when we see our spouses—after years of marriage—make decisions that are different from their usual routines. *Who is this man I thought I had figured out?* I think of my own husband. *Who is this man doing his own laundry? Who is this man disappearing for hours on end to ride his bike? Who is this man reaching out to hold my hand more often?*

We really can have two responses to such changes. We can be alarmed, reeling a bit in fright of a relationship we are far less in control of than we first assumed, or it can invigorate us, fanning the flame of love as we realize there is still more left to discover in our partners. What once seemed commonplace now has a spark of mystery. We are intrigued.

The same is true of our interactions with the Divine. Will we grow fearful and suspicious, or will we be projected into a new spiritual dimension, a new awakening, a new relationship with the One we thought we had figured out. Are we willing to be surprised? Or, the even bigger question is, are we willing to wait for the next surprise without floundering and flipping out in the meantime?

I think it's the times in between revelations that really test our faith. I've experienced this with God. Faith has become dead or commonplace. I have simply lost connection with "It." Can I have the peace of mind to wait for my next encounter with Him? To know that even though I don't feel Him now in my life, His presence is just as sure as it has ever been. Can I trust that He is just arranging His next surprise? I must simply wait for the breathtaking unveiling. For it is as God in the book *The Shack* said: "I have a great fondness for uncertainty."[2]

This waiting room is where I seem to spend most of my time. It is the place of questions and hurt and depression and puzzling scenarios that cannot be solved. It is the place where doubts are born and where I start to wonder, *Am I just making this whole God thing up completely? Why can't I be happy? Content?* The waiting room requires us to slow down, to be patient, to rest in what we do know of the character of God. It asks us to draw on our limited images of Him and believe that He will come to us again and in a new way that will both illuminate and outgrow all the other images combined. The Divine is mystery, and though that is maddening, it's what keeps our hearts alive, our souls breathing. It is God without an agenda, at least without our agenda. It is God as friend. It is God so big and shifting, He must exist apart from us, and yet somehow He is able to still reside in us.

The problem I have had with Christianity lately is that it has become commonplace to me. I have learned to define God by certain imagery, with certain words, and they have been the same images and words for years. I have come to harbor a deep shame inside me for believing those images were dead.

I kept trying to kneel over top of them and blow my breath through their pale blue lips, but they just weren't springing back to life. I tried to stand in front of them so no one would notice how still they were lying. Occasionally I would lift a hand of one of the images and wave it, much like Woody does with Buzz Lightyear's unattached arm in the first *Toy Story* movie. I would lean out from around the window and wave the dead arm of my godly images so that other Christians would think my faith was still vibrant, my God still alive.

I wasn't doing it to be deceitful as much as I was doing it hopefully, supposing that maybe this time the arm really would come back to life when I waved it. I was desperate for that to happen, for who would understand if I told them I had killed God? Who would believe me that it had happened quite by accident when I wasn't looking? Who would understand my embarrassment? Who was a safe person to admit all this to? Who could I tell that wouldn't respond with trite answers like "Try harder to feel Him and obey His commandments. Get rid of the sin in your life and redouble your efforts and read your Bible more to find the answers"?

I wondered if anyone else was hiding their own God-corpse, pretending that He was still alive and well, pausing once in a while when no one was looking to blow air into those pale blue lips. Crossing their fingers for unknown reasons and hoping that this time there would be some semblance of movement. A flutter of eyelashes, a stirring of the fingers. Something.

But there was nothing. Time and time again there was nothing. At least not there. Not in those dead images, dead words, dead actions. It was about this time that I was reading the novel *Frankenstein*, and I caught glimpses of God's clothing, supposing God has to wear clothes at all, as He darted in and out of the sentences of that book. *Was that Him?* I would wonder, rubbing my eyes and pinching them shut, shaking my head to make sure I was thinking straight. I would read on in *Frankenstein*:

> There is something at work in my soul which I do not understand.... There is a love for the marvellous, a belief in the marvellous, intertwined in all my projects, which hurries me out of the common pathways of men, even to the wild sea and unvisited regions I am about to explore.[3]

And there out of the corner of my eye, I would catch movement again. My heart was racing. Movement. Life.

I peered over my shoulder at the corpse. I wondered if it was possible that God had moved on. Does He do that? Does He depart one image and pour Himself into another? What if He does? What if He is the kind of God who would show up where I need to see Him simply because my heart has longing? What if the longing—masquerading as embarrassment for the lifeless corpse—is actually the ushering in of the Divine? What if I've carried my longing into this book, and He is flirting with me here? How scandalous to think of a God who flirts with me, and yet I've seen too much to back down now. I am lured.

"I'll bite," I say, suspiciously, expectantly, like a nervous lover glancing anxiously across the room at another who keeps making eye contact with her. I am blushing, and He, He is walking toward me. He is making no mistake about it. His actions are clear. He is coming for me. Darting in and out of the words now, much like people in a crowded room, showing Himself more and more. Whatever will I do when He approaches me, and everyone knows He's picked me? What will I do when they see me dancing with this new image, and they become aware that there is a corpse I have abandoned entirely? My face is so hot I feel it might consume me completely.

This is the mystery. The mystery that the actual road we pick doesn't matter as long as there is longing, a heart seeking to find Him. A heart haunted by the desire for life to the full, for love that completes us, for joy that sustains us even while we sit with corpses strewn across our laps in crowded waiting rooms. As God said in *The Shack*, "I will travel any road to find you."[4] And He will, and He did, and He does. And it is He who then woos us onto unique, personal, narrow roads that few have traveled.

About a year ago, Tony and I started a small group, or life group, as our church calls them. The purpose of a life group in a church as big as ours is to have a small, intimate group of people to connect with, to do life with. We met on Wednesday nights, and it was made up of three other couples. Sometimes we would get together with our families for dinner or playdates outside of that Wednesday-night commitment. It was a great group.

But very slowly I started noticing myself not wanting to attend. I wasn't looking forward to it like I used to. I didn't feel like I had much to contribute to the conversation. It felt rather forced and empty to me. And I felt as if I was being a horrible friend for wanting out. How could all these rebellious feelings be rising in me? What was wrong with me?

I mentioned it to Tony. I told him I didn't think I could do it anymore.

"I feel like I'm pretending. Like I'm going through the motions for something I don't believe in. I'm just not passionate about the Bible right now like they all are. I'm just not in the serving and churchgoing and praying together mind-set."

"Let's give it some time," he said. "We started the group. I don't want to just bail. Let me talk to them about it."

He didn't get a chance to talk to them. One of the couples was in another life group, and they were feeling the strain of overcommitment. They sent a message out to our group that they would be leaving our group to focus solely on their other one.

"It's my out," I told Tony. "It's the perfect time to dissolve the group."

He agreed and let me write a note to the group explaining that we needed to stop meeting as well. I felt free. I felt so free that I decided maybe God wanted me to start another life group. One specifically for artists. I mentioned it to Teresa.

"Why?" she asked.

"Because I want to be around like-minded people," I replied off the cuff.

"Do you have to have a life group for that? I mean, what would you do in your life group?"

"Um, I'm not sure. I hadn't really thought about it. I just was thinking I probably need to be in one so I don't ..." My voice trailed off. I realized exactly what I was doing. I was trying to replace one rule with another. I was feeling the urge to fulfill my church's desire to have me in a life group. I was people pleasing, performing, rule following. I was feeling guilty that I wasn't in church, wasn't reading my Bible, and now wasn't in a life group. Surely I was going to slip into Satan's lair for eternity. Much like I rushed to wanting to serve in the nursery when I stopped going to church, now I wanted to rush into a new life group to replace the old one.

I looked at Teresa. "I probably don't need to rush into starting a life group, I'd be doing it for all the wrong reasons."

"I don't want to discourage you. Maybe it's something you do down the road," she said warmly.

I was having to come to terms with the fact that I had another lifeless corpse lying at my feet, this one by the name of *life group*. It was so hard to not want to give up on God altogether.

I met over coffee a month or two later with one of the women from that life group. She informed me that they were starting to meet again, and that they had invited some other couples. A twinge of disappointment signaled within me. *See what you're missing? You gave up a really good thing.* But then I remembered how fake I felt sitting in each other's living rooms, trying to drum up some energy to discuss the scripture from last week's message that I didn't hear.

"Part of me wishes I could do the life group thing," I told her, "but I just can't right now. I miss getting to be with you all as friends, but discussing spiritual things was getting a little tiresome. I felt like the broken record, always pulling the discussion away from where it was naturally meant to go. I can only say so many times that Galatians is the only part of the Bible I care to read, and I don't really care for church right now. It's like I just don't have much in common, which really isn't anybody's fault. It just is what it is."

I was overexplaining myself. I wished I could keep my words in my mouth, but I felt it necessary to defend my actions. My friend said words of grace that washed over me.

"It's fine," she said. Or "I understand," she said. Or "I think that's so brave of you," she said. She got it.

This must be what it feels like to agree to disagree, I thought. *To peaceably decide to go in two different directions.* Part of me wanted to convince her that she didn't need a life group either. Was it possible that she was trapped in the religion of it like me? And yet she had such peace about the life-group thing. She seemed to enjoy it, even desire it.

We sipped on lattes and talked about messy faith and jobs and being moms and being women. I felt camaraderie, companionship, and a gentle coaxing to go on and do the things God was stirring in me. To write my book, to write my confusion, to write—in some scatterbrained attempt—about the mystery. I felt a bit sloppy around my edges, but safe to be so in her presence.

As we stood to leave, I felt as if we were standing at a split in the narrow road. As if we were being forced to unlink hands so she could go off to the left and I could go off a bit to the right. It was unnerving to let go of that desire to travel with someone else. A bit unnerving to watch her go around a bend and wonder if she was right and I was wrong. Should I sprint after her? Should I holler out, "No, wait! I was wrong. Wait for me. I'm coming with you"? I sure wished her way would work for me. It would be easier that way. Much easier.

We are all of us desperate, at some time or another, to institutionalize God, build structures, construct ideologies, and devise formulas that will make Him certain and secure, attainable and controllable. We are seeking certain paths for our own comfort. But the Divine will not be chained down. And this is the haunted beauty of it all. That He is always revealing Himself in present terms, always in the now.

God is not limited to who He was and God is not limited to who He will be. God is "I AM." God is relevant *now* in ways that can meet our hearts' needs. God is alive and on the move and flirting with us. Can we lift our eyes from the container in which we once found Him and delight in a mystery that rarely will find Him in the same place twice?

If we could but see our longing and our hurting and our haunting and our inadequacies as invitations to His beauty and power and love. If we could just see our ugly-duckling feathers and thick eyeliner as invitations into the unknown land of swanhood. Oh, that we might, as Gerald May states in *Addiction and Grace*, "recognize our incompleteness as a kind of spaciousness into which we can welcome the flow of grace."[5]

Last night I found myself in the dark place again. I found myself unable to parent, unable to laugh, unable to feel anything desirable about life. I felt cheated again of my life to the full. I morbidly wondered, sitting in the car, numb, as Tony drove our family to eat supper at a friend's house, if this is how Virginia Woolf felt before she committed suicide. Like no matter how hard she tried to see purpose and meaning in life and to connect with some source of happiness, the light kept getting snuffed out. I wonder how many times one tries to light it again? What good is there in continuing on?

Walt Whitman answers me tonight: "That the powerful play goes on, and you will contribute a verse."[6] With breath still in my lungs, I can only contribute *my* verse. And as I sat last night in a dark backyard for a Fourth of July celebration, I witnessed Japanese lanterns being lit from within and rising up, up, up into the night. And I thought to myself, *I still have a spark. I still feel that pilot light blazing, somewhere, deep in me. I am lighter than air. I am lighter than this dark dungeon that threatens me. The mystery means there is something more to be discovered, so why would I quit now?*

I feel like Jeremiah again. I am a prophetess, and as bleak as things get, I can't seem to give up. "But if I say, 'Forget it! No more GOD-Messages from me!' the words are fire in my belly, a burning in my bones. I'm worn out trying to hold it in. I can't do it any longer!" (Jer. 20:9 MSG). I concur with Jeremiah that there is unspeakable light within, and it's scampering around in search of a release valve.

Chapter Twelve

Love

I have done a lot of crazy things in the name of love. I've purchased gifts for boys—random gifts like Notre Dame T-shirts, gold jewelry, and plastic trolls with naked butts and fuzzy blue hair. I've taken alternate paths down school hallways just to be sure I would *accidentally* bump into a special someone. I have worn outfits I didn't entirely like, such as shin-length dresses with gawdy floral patterns and uncomfortable shoulder pads, because I could tell this is what people I loved preferred, and I wanted them to love me back. I have said yes when I wanted to say no and have said no when I so badly wanted to say yes.

I've entered into exercise programs and educational programs and religious programs to show my serious affection for others. To let them know that I hear their voices, and I appreciate their wisdom. I have baked meals, babysat children, and attended social events so that others might feel loved. I've answered emails and texts, responded to blog comments and Facebook updates, written thank-yous, and changed my entire schedule so that I could prove my love. I've acquired new musical interests or new artistic interests or new athletic interests or new political interests in my own desperate desire for love. I have avoided conflict, made peace, silenced my voice, and outperformed my own limitations so I could prove myself lovable. I have followed protocol, status quo, and general consensus in order to be loved and to show love.

As I'm sitting here today thinking about love, I realize that throughout my life, many times the driving factor of my love has been fear. A desperate fear that if I don't maintain X, Y, or Z, love will be snatched away from me. A sick assumption that if I am not the one to work for love and chase after it, love will slip forever out of reach. A misconstrued view that love requires sacrifice of everything that is truly me, a giving up of my dreams and my likes and my desires and my instincts. I have come to see love as doing the opposite of what I wish to do. A dying to self that has nearly killed me. And as I type this, all I can hear in the back of my mind is a soft whispering of "perfect love casts out fear" (1 John 4:18 NKJV).

I have known my entire life that God is love. I have been told my entire life through sing-song and otherwise that "Jesus loves me." So why am I, at thirty-two years of age, sitting here admitting on paper that I have rarely ever felt loved and certainly have rarely ever acted out of pure love for another? I suppose it's because knowing in your head and knowing in your heart are two disconnected things sometimes. And while my head has been inundated with messages of love and formulas to prove love, protect love, and control love, my heart has seldom felt free enough to engage in the type of love God supposedly offers me.

I think my sudden interest in real love has come from two places. First, I had completely ceased to feel any sort of love from or for God; and second, I felt completely burned out to be able to give love or receive love from any of the people around me. Feeling completely inept at maintaining all the performance that I contributed to receiving love and giving love, I suddenly understood how powerful it would be if God could first love me, rather than me having to love Him. What if I could do nothing, for I had no strength or desire to do anything anymore, and was still loved by God? What then?

I had built my whole life around my activity being equivalent to my lovableness. Religions are built on this sort of devotion. And yet, I wondered if it was possible to stop loving as I have known it and still be loved in return.

Meister Eckhart said once, "Good company can also hinder him—not just the street, but the church, too; not only evil words and deeds, but good words and deeds as well. For the hindrance is in him, because in him God has not become all things."[1]

This is clearly the crossroads I have come to. The problem is not the church or the Bible or the religion or how I was raised; the problem is my tainted view of love. The problem exists inside me. God is not love to me, and if God's love isn't enough for me, no one's is.

It's all so very dreamlike when I try to put it down on paper, like mist slipping through my fingers. I want to document it so as to share it, but I fear it isn't like the formulas I've sought out my whole life. It is far more intimate and mysterious and intangible than a formula or proof will ever be, and the road to get here is simply not paved with any clear intention of my own. It's as though I have been the delightful victim of a rescuing, and I can only hope the powers that be may initiate other great rescues on the lives of those who read this, for it is by far the most poignant time I have ever experienced thus far in my life.

I have alluded already in this book to spending a year reading Galatians. This came riding on the shirttails of reading *Frankenstein* and surprisingly and happily finding God there. I hadn't been reading the Bible at all at the time, but a friend of mine shared a passage with me from Galatians, and it spoke to my desire to be an artist, so I was somehow able to hear the words separately from the dreadful religion I was nailed to. I think it helped that the version of the Bible was one I wasn't familiar with—*The Message*—so it didn't strike me as the Bible but rather as some book I had never read or heard tell of.

The passage read, "Make a careful exploration of who you are and the work you have been given, and then sink yourself into that. Don't be impressed with yourself. Don't compare yourself with others. Each of you must take responsibility for doing the creative best you can with your own life" (Gal. 6:4–5 MSG).

Even now as I read it, I'm floored with the freedom that it stirs within me. As I read it nearly a year and a half ago, I felt God giving me permission to do what I longed to do. At that point I wasn't at complete burnout, but I was very tired of thinking I had to live a certain way to prove my love for God. And I was very tired of stuffing this desire to be an artist, feeling I needed to save it for a time when my kids and others in my life didn't need me.

What I read in these magical words of Galatians, whether I knew it or not at the time, was an invitation to retrust God, to take Him at His word, to believe that He really did love me and He really did have my best interest in mind. What felt like a rebellious and selfish step toward self-gratification was something else entirely. It was the resparking of a romance I had completely forgotten. I jumped into Galatians to fall in love with art and with myself, and I walked out of Galatians (although I will never walk out of it entirely) a year later totally in love with God again. Galatians didn't change all of my performance addictions, but it did wake me up to their existence, and it gave me the grace to be loved regardless.

Grace would be the word that summed up Galatians for me, and grace would lead me to love. Which is where I feel I am now. An ever-increasing awareness of love. A love for myself like I had never known, a love for the Divine, who is somehow both bigger than I am and yet is inside me. A love for my husband that is fresh and different and so much less concerned with his performance or my own.

What I'm finding about love is it shows up in many different forms, in many different ways, and my capacity to love and be loved is ever changing and increasing. It's almost painful, right now, to receive love apart from performance. I feel like the exchange rate is unfair. I haven't given you anything (because I have nothing left of me to give), so how could I possibly accept this love from you? But I'm doing it anyway, because I realize how badly I need to be loved for me, not loved for my actions.

My actions have fallen away. I'm not cooking meals for my friends who have new babies, and I'm fighting off the voices that tell me my friends will no longer love me. I'm not attending social events that I don't want to go to, and the demons of performance are attacking me viciously, telling me I am a loner, telling me I will have no friends. I'm not going to church or offering to watch my friends' kids or rushing in to save the day when people say they need me.

I haven't seen my sweet neighbor friend across the street for over a week. Every time I leave my house, I look at her house and think, *She probably believes I'm a horrible friend. Why don't I ever make time for her?* I imagine her standing at her front window, shaking her head at me as I back out of my driveway. Her hands are on her hips, her long hair falls in soft curls along the sides of her neck, shifting its weight as she shakes her head in disapproval. I imagine her writing my name down on a list that is taped over her living room couch, something titled: "People to Unfriend" or "People to Never Trust Again" or "People Who Flat-out Annoy Me." I think it's possible I may have a problem with paranoia.

One night I was meeting with Teresa at Starbucks. We managed to snag our big, comfy chairs that night, and they were pulled close so we could share creative secrets.

"It's so hard to know whether I should commit to something or not. My choices are all so subconsciously mixed in with people pleasing and God pleasing that I can't ever tell if my motives are pure."

"Here, grab your pen," she said, holding it out to me. "I want you to write this down. Write it somewhere you can refer back to, like maybe here." She opened up the front cover of my journal—I always have a journal with me—and motioned toward the inside front cover.

"Do I have the grace for this?" I transcribed the words as she spoke them to me.

"Oh, and add this too," she said. "No is a complete sentence."

I stared at the phrases. I thought about how strange it was that I had never used the front cover of my journals. I vowed to do so from now on. Magic words belong there, and these seemed like magic words to me, as if spoken from an oracle.

Now I am taking each item that requires my action, and I am asking myself, *Do I have the grace to do this? Would I be doing this to prove my love because I'm scared that if I don't I won't be loved in return, or am I doing this out of a pure desire?* Most things, right now anyway, I'm doing out of fear of others, so I'm covering myself in God's grace and saying no to a lot of what others want from me and yes to a lot of what I want for myself. It feels selfish yet liberating. It feels un-Christian, yet it allows me to breathe, and these days, breathing continuous, unhurried, unhindered breaths feels like quite an accomplishment. I keep getting inner assurance that this is for a season. That someday, much like an alcoholic, I may be able to dine in a restaurant that offers alcohol on the menu and not feel threatened that I might overindulge. However, in my current state, it's best if I just stay out of the restaurant entirely.

Everything has threads of performance tied to it, and I have to cut away a thread at a time. The threads are the consistency of spiderwebs, not hard to break once you see them, but often invisible to the naked eye unless the light hits them just so. I don't know how many threads are attached to me, but I know that the Divine can shine light on them as I need to see them. As I break them, I can feel them wrap their sticky residue around my wrist or my neck, an eerie remnant reminding me of how imprisoning or choking these threads can be when left unnoticed. They cling to me, trying to convince me I will walk unbalanced without them. That they, in fact, are the strength that holds me up. But I know the stumbling is just momentary, and I will regain my footing with time. The thing about new-found freedom is that it looks oddly a lot like chaos, something an overachieving, people-pleasing perfectionist would just as soon avoid. But I'm learning to embrace the messy for what it brings, and what it brings is change. To stay the same is to kill the soul and strangle the mystery of the Divine. To change is to always awake to the new and, thus, to always be slightly off balance, to always be slightly messy. Love is messy.

I am a big fan of the artist Keri Smith. She has written a book titled *Mess*, and when I read the introduction, I can translate it into what I'm learning about love. She speaks to the idea that before a fall, there is this invigorating moment when we decide we're going to let go and try something new. I imagine it's much like a baby taking his or her first steps.

I'm suddenly trying to walk around without these spiderwebs of performance to balance me, and I'm stumbling a little in the dark, like the first drunk woman I saw years ago as I left the stadium after a Cincinnati Reds baseball game. Her legs were rubbery, unsure, like a marionette dipping and swaying jerkily. I've always associated this feeling with that of failure, someone acting the fool. I've always thought this sort of imbalance was a sign I had gotten off course. But Keri Smith turns my world on its head when she asks me, "What does if feel like to throw yourself off balance on purpose?"[2]

"Are you crazy?" I want to sneer at her. "Why would I go and do a thing like that?"

But I know doing so will take me somewhere I've never been.

New and different. This is what I want, isn't it? To know the Divine in a new and different way? To explore ever-expanding mystery? To understand a love that is completely new and different from any I have ever known? To relax and enjoy the flow?

In my religious pursuits, I've taken to making things perfect. In doing so, what I'm missing is the playful exploration. Getting to the end becomes more important than the means. I have to offer up this perfect, pristine, sacrificial love for those around me. That's what I thought my God required of me. So in order to do this, it didn't matter whether I was enjoying what I was doing. It didn't matter whether I was passionate or engaged in the process. It didn't matter whether it was silently killing me. All that mattered is that the end result came across as a perfect love. The end is more important than the means. The performance strings of my web gave me the appearance of a balanced love. I felt stable because everything looked as it should. I received pats on the back and penciled-in stars on my measuring wall.

But things are also getting pretty mundane. I feel as if I'm going through the motions. I feel as if I'm pretending that I'm feeling any sort of love in return. It sucks to pretend.

Keri's suggestions feel unsafe, rebellious, even foolish. Keri is challenging me to engage without worrying about the outcome. I gasp. Could this be how God loves me? Could this be the definition of unconditional love?

She is asking me to trust the process. To enjoy the process. To do by instinct without worrying about the end result.

Oh, God. No. I can't let the final product out of my sight, can I? Would my neighbor still love me if a week went by without our interaction? Would You still love me if I couldn't step through a church's doors without feeling a bit squeamish? Would my husband still love me if he had to walk downstairs for a pair of his clean jeans or if there were no supper prepared tonight when he returns from work? Would my homeschool co-op still love me if I couldn't teach another art class? Would my parents still love me if I couldn't make it home for Christmas?

Every time I go to love, I'm thinking about the end result. I'm thinking about how to give the appearance of a perfect, polished love that keeps everyone happy. But what if I could love with weak knees, stumbling a bit over my own two feet like the drunk woman? What if I could love in ways I never thought I was capable of simply because I'm doing things I never thought I was allowed to do? What if it didn't seem like such an atrocity to love myself?

Am I allowed to experiment with love like Keri Smith experiments with art? How messy am I allowed to make things? How many times can one fall and still retain some sort of equanimity? Am I failing or am I learning?

Is love unpredictable? Do I need to be in control of the outcome, or can I trust the Divine with that? Can love show up unexpectedly like the happy accidents we find in art? Do I want a love that is programmable, or do I want love to come in like a train, rattling through the tunnel of my best passionate attempts and sweeping me off my feet in a burst of glory? Do I want to love others in the same old calculated way, or do I want my love to bend and blow deep in the winds of life, a piece of Oklahoma winter wheat dancing to some rhythm unheard by common ears?

Chapter Thirteen

Childlike

My oldest daughter recently decided she wanted to be baptized. Elated, Tony and I talked to her about what that meant, wanting to make sure she understood the commitment she was making. Turns out, I think she understood it better than I do, especially in this confusing place I am in my faith right now.

Tony and I had this fleeting moment when we wondered if she was too young, at seven years old, to truly grasp the concept of brokenness and salvation and redemption, but as we asked her questions about her faith, we realized we were in error, and it would be foolish for us to talk her out of something she believed so profusely. I was stunned by how simple her faith was and how complicated mine had become.

I have to be honest, I was a bit torn watching her make a decision I wasn't sure I agreed with anymore. A question came to mind that I had heard my father-in-law pose one time when faced with some of life's challenges: "Do I really believe in all this Jesus stuff?" I was too confused to know. I think my relationship used to be with

Jesus, and I was scared of God and scared of not living up to and performing all the rules of my religion. Now my relationship is with God, and I'm scared of Jesus. Scared of His call to suffer, to sacrifice, to die to self. One of my biggest stumbling blocks to believing and trusting right now is my inability to explain any of this to anyone. If I believe in this Jesus stuff, I can't defend it or lead someone else to Christ, because it doesn't make sense to me. If I can't explain it, why would I believe it myself? (Especially when a good Christian's main purpose seems to be to evangelize.)

I wasn't going to church at the time, and I wondered if I was being a hypocrite watching my daughter get baptized in a church I wasn't attending (despite the fact that my husband was on staff there). I also wondered if I should let her commit to something that felt so complicated and messy to me. But as I journaled, writing my concerns to God, I realized she should be allowed to make her own decision. She was excited to make this decision, and she was excited to make it in church, where some of her friends could cheer her on. This was not about me; this was about her, and she was undoubtedly ready for it. And complicated as faith may be, I was still very much in favor of encouraging a relationship with God. After all, my relationship with God was the only thing keeping me sane. If this made Him feel more real to her, then so be it.

There is a scene in the movie *Ratatouille* where the food critic sits in the restaurant waiting to be impressed. He is critical and doubtful, but he sits there nonetheless. When the food finally gets delivered and he takes a bite, the scene flashes back to his childhood, where he sits as a little boy at the dinner table eating the delicious and love-infused ratatouille his own mother had prepared for him. He is overcome with emotion at the vivid memory.[1] As I tearfully watched Tony and our daughter enter the large plastic pool filled with warm water, I was thrust into my own emotional flashback.

I saw myself, as a little girl, after my own baptism on Easter Day. I was about four years older than Zoe when she chose to be baptized, and I was sitting on the curb with my new Bible, reading crazy stories in the book of Revelation of pregnant women and dragons to any passing neighbors who would listen. As I looked at myself as a child, I wondered if I was mad at or embarrassed by or disappointed in that little Mandy. It was strange getting the fortunate chance to meet little Mandy through my daughter Zoe, because I realized how much I loved that little version of me, purely covered in all sorts of grace. On the morning she was to get baptized, Zoe had told me, "Mama, there is something hopping in me happy," and I realized there had been something hopping happy in that little Mandy, too.

"The angels are rejoicing in heaven," my mom told me as she clasped a tiny gold cross around my neck, a gift for my baptism.

The little Mandy liked mystery. She believed. She didn't know enough to be ashamed. There was nothing to be ashamed of. It's okay for kids to believe wild things. Faulty theology was acceptable. It wasn't even questioned. Faith was cute. My little relationship with God was still pure, motivated from a loving heart rather than a guilty conscience and the need to prove myself. At some point, though, God lost His glimmer and even became a bit embarrassing. I took my eyes off Him, or rather my eyes became cloudy, scaled, unable to see Him clearly. He became disfigured, stern, a taskmaster. He looked a little like my dad and a little like my mom; a little like my short, mustached, slightly balding minister at my childhood church;

a little like coaches and teachers and mentors and professors who all had their opinions on life and how it should be led. He looked like church camp and Christian movies. He became a bit awkward and foolish and clueless, and so did I, because I believed in a God who was such.

A couple of days after Zoe was baptized, she had a breakdown. She was hurt about something, a fight she had gotten into with her siblings. As I sat on the bottom bunk bed with her and held her hand, she admitted something to me that took my breath away: "I don't feel any different. I'm supposed to have Jesus in me now, but I feel exactly the same. I still get sad. I still get mad. Nothing changed."

In my head, I defaulted into "I've been a Christian all my life" mode. *These things just can't be said. What atrocities. You're questioning the very root of Christianity. Of course you're changed. Of course things are different. Don't speak such things. Just believe. Just smile and nod and be a nice girl.*

How easy it is to spout off the prescribed "right answers." To say, "It just is this way because I told you so." But she's right, you know? My Zoe is right. I remember thinking the same thing as a child, a sense of dread that my baptism didn't take or that maybe I was immune to the supposed magic.

I didn't have a good answer for her. How could I? I didn't have a good answer for myself.

"That feels so frustrating, doesn't it?" I said to her, stalling, aching, wishing I had more to offer.

"Yes," she said, rubbing her wet eyes and sighing deeply.

"I don't quite understand it all either, Zoe. I really think you had Jesus with you all along, and that this baptism was a ceremony to outwardly celebrate that with your friends and your family. It's a way of saying you believe what Jesus taught. That you love Him and want to live a life like His. Having a relationship with God doesn't mean your life is going to be easy or that you're going to be perfect and happy all the time. Maybe having God inside you means He's close enough to give you second chances every time you feel defeated and you just want to give up like this,"

She smiled at me weakly. I smiled back weakly. *We have years and years of this to come,* I thought. *Plenty more God-sized conversations to walk through that I have no answers for.* But there is a great comfort in just being able to say, "I'm not sure." There is a great comfort in being able to admit there is some mystery to it all, and I simply choose to believe anyway.

Several months later, I noticed Zoe sitting on the black couch in our living room with her Bible open on her lap. She looked dejected.

"What's wrong?" I asked.

"They tell me in church I'm supposed to read this. They tell me I should read it every day. That if I read it, I'll know God better. I want to know God better, but I haven't been reading it every day. I forget. Or some days I just don't want to."

She gets it, I thought. *She gets it, and she's so young. She's processing some of the same things I'm processing. She's not too ashamed to say them out loud. Thank You, God, that she's not ashamed to say them, and that I have words to encourage her on this subject.*

"Zoe, you don't have to read your Bible every day. That book is filled with all sorts of amazing stories; many of them are fascinating. But you don't have to read them every single day. You read the Bible when you feel excited about reading the Bible, and on the days you don't, or when you forget, or when you just didn't get to it, you can look for God to show up in other areas of your life. You can get to know Him better by chasing butterflies outside or by laughing with your sister or by eating a strawberry. God is in everything, and if you're paying attention, He'll reveal Himself to you in all sorts of ways.

"Don't feel bad because you didn't read your Bible and you were told to. God isn't upset with you. He's not disappointed. He's so thrilled that your heart wants to know Him and connect with Him."

She was relieved—elated, actually. She reminded me of something I had told her before, that God is an artist, and His creations show up all over the place.

Last week Zoe told me she was reading Esther.

"Oh yeah? How is it?" I asked.

"It's so good, Mom. There is this man, and he wants to kill people, and then there is beautiful Esther, who is a queen, a *real* queen, and …"

Her voice was passionate as she relayed the story to me. I found myself intrigued.

"Maybe I'll read Esther too," I said, interrupting her briefly. "It sounds so good."

"Oh, it is, Mommy. It's such a good story." She continued to talk about it, skipping along behind me as we loaded scooters and helmets and water bottles into the car for a park trip.

She's reading the Bible because she wants to, I told myself. *How wonderful.*

This is a big change from the dejected "I'm failing, and I need to read it because I was told to at church." Zoe's engaged and learning and finding her own beauty there. God is revealing Himself to her through a good story.

Isn't that where we always find Him? Woven through intense plots, where dark and light collide? Sometimes in the Bible. Sometimes in real life. Sometimes in *Frankenstein*. Because narrow-path people know we've got to keep our own stories with God alive, no matter what it takes. And sometimes that means reading our Bibles, and sometimes that means taking a break. And sometimes that means admitting the way we thought it should work just isn't working.

Is God the good guy or the bad guy?

Is He safe?

Sometimes it means admitting that this baptism thing isn't all it's cracked up to be. Admitting that the plot is thickening and the mystery is increasing, and I'm a little scared and a little angry and a little shaken up by the whole thing. Maybe that's precisely what we need to fan the flame of faith. To see the richness in our own ebbing and flowing story lines. Don't we all have a taste for adventure, a longing for things not to be as they once seemed?

Zoe's baptism awakened more questions in me, but it also reminded me of a warm and loving place where it was easy to believe. It reminded me of a simplicity of faith that I had lost. I wondered if, as an adult, I could ever have that back.

Chapter Fourteen

Belong

May you never be isolated. May you always be in
the gentle nest of belonging with your *anam cara*.

—John O'Donohue, *Anam Cara*

When it comes down to it, I really just want to feel like I belong
somewhere. I want to feel that the deeper internal parts of me—
what we might equate to my soul—are not freakish or screwed
up but are useful to God. I want to believe that I can connect to
humanity on a level that really matters, a level where I am fully
known and loved.

John O'Donohue says in his book *Anam Cara*, "All our inner
life and intimacy of soul longs to find an outer mirror. It longs for a
form in which it can be seen, felt, and touched."[1] I realize part of this
journey for me has been in search of an outer mirror. Maybe it's my
growing artistic voice that is looking for an outlet. Let me find a mirror big enough to express all the swirling emotions and frustrations

and passions inside of me. Let me find a mirror that is big enough to reflect the Divine who is living inside me. It seems my problem is that I've outgrown all my outer mirrors, and in my impatience, I've started to question whether my faith is even real. If I can't explain it or express it or defend it, is it still real?

Digging into philosophy has been good for me. I've enjoyed the mental gymnastics that it requires to wrap my head around things like Zen and mysticism. However, there are times, as I mentioned before, when I think myself in circles until I'm dizzy. Yesterday was one of those days. Yesterday I fell apart, crying on my husband's shoulder, shaking as I told him, "I don't even know what I believe anymore. I want to believe in Jesus, but I don't know if I do. I want to believe I have a relationship with God and I hear from Him, but sometimes I feel like I'm just going crazy."

Does anyone else hear the things I'm hearing? The question is too scary to ask out loud.

Tony held me. He wrapped his strong arms around me and just let me cry. I didn't feel him fidget impatiently. I felt him solid. There for me.

I am so thankful I haven't felt it necessary to burn the bridge between us so that I can find myself. There is strength and healing in Tony's arms. They aren't smothering; they are simply available. He's letting me explore, experiment, question, and writhe. He's not rushing in to solve me. He's giving me a protective place to get messy.

The closer I get to God, the less I understand, and the less understanding seems to matter at all. Am I going crazy longing for something I can't explain? I want to belong with Him. I want to believe I am loved and accept it. I want to settle in. I want to stop picking His love apart and just relax into it. I'm tired of striving so hard to get things right.

I read two more quotes from *Anam Cara*, a book I'm currently enjoying immensely.

"Their relationship consisted in discussing if it existed."[2]

"If you keep shining the neon light of analysis and accountability on the tender tissue of your belonging, you make it parched and barren."[3]

I am realizing that I'm trying to talk myself out of God's love and friendship. *What if it isn't what I think it is?* I want to move past this before I kill the little shoot of love that is just beginning to bloom. I want to just enjoy this love and friendship for what it is currently and be grateful for it. I don't want to be isolated anymore. I want to trust.

I remember the day Tony and I were on a date. We were driving toward the sunset. The sky was orange and pink and soft.

"I think I have trust issues," I said, bursting through the silence like the sun's pastel rays were bursting through the clouds.

He seemed caught off guard. Laughing abruptly, he replied, "You and me both."

"So how is it that we manage to make this thing work?" I said, motioning back and forth between myself and him.

"Because we don't play games with each other. We know that with each other, we don't have any hidden agendas or manipulating attempts to say one thing while meaning another."

"I'm glad we have each other," I said.

"So am I. Many times my relationship with you is the only one that seems to work."

I can't stop thinking about my trust issues, though. I'm always thinking, *I must look out for myself, because if I don't no one will.* I am constantly on the defense, looking for—and at times probably creating—instances where people are trying to take advantage of me, mock me, or fix me. The result comes across as a woman engaging with others at arm's length, for fear that their misunderstandings of me and their disagreements with me will result in my becoming someone I'm not. I've worked so hard the past few months to detach myself from performance that I'm scared to be around people for fear I'll instantly start performing to fulfill their desires again. And yet I am lonely for companionship, for community, for a place to share this overwhelming love of God that keeps welling up within me.

The past two to three months or so, I had really become a recluse, turning inward and spending precious alone time with God. I had stopped going to church, stopped interacting socially, stopped blogging and engaging with other social media. I had created my own little cabin in the woods where I could come to know God in ways that were intimate and unlike anything I had experienced in the history of my faith.

The past two weeks I've felt God begin to release me from this "time alone." Slowly He has been unweaving me, as if I had been a dancer tucked into His arms, and now He is sending me in a twirl to unwind back into the "real world."

It has been tumultuous, because I'm entering old territory as a new person, and I'm having trouble trusting that my new persona is strong enough to exist around others. I keep looking back at the God I have come to know with a sort of *verklempt* expression, asking, "Do

I really need all these other people? Couldn't it just be You and me and forget everyone else?" People confused me.

I believe God reminded me of something, though. He reminded me that while I don't technically *need* others, in the sense that God fully completes me and fulfills all desires for love inside me, I do still have a desire for human companionship. I long for the outer to mirror the inner. For people to see an outward reflection of all that is transpiring inside of me. It's something I long to share, long to express, long to process with other human beings who exist in the mess of trying to live a life to the fullest. Maybe it's because I'm an artist, or maybe it's just because God created His love to overflow from person to person to person so that we might all be connected and have a sense of belonging.

I need a tangible place to express the intangible internal lessons. I need to experience outwardly the me I know I am inwardly. I can't do this without human interaction.

God reminded me of something else as well. It is often in rubbing shoulders with humanity that we come to see God in a new light. His creation always speaks of Him, and we are a part of His creation. For instance, I feel very strongly that God sent me my friendship with Teresa during this dark time in my life so I would have a physical representation ever before me of His love for me. In so many ways, my relationship with her allowed me to make God's love and acceptance of me tangible.

There were times when it was hard for me to open up to her and trust her, and these mirrored the times I was having trouble opening up to and trusting God. There were some times I even wondered if her friendship was a figment of my imagination; it was so raw and pure, it seemed impossible it could be real. Perhaps I had created her in my mind simply because I needed the concrete example of the feminine side of God.

But no, she was real. A gift. And she was the one I texted the day I had to go in for an unexpected church meeting.

"The two guys that are sort of over Tony on his team at work have asked Tony and me to come in to talk," I told her, my fingers nervously, anxiously searching for the proper letters on my iPhone.

"They haven't seen me in church recently, and they are worried about me." I texted the words sitting on the edge of my bed, fumbling for my shoes. I felt as if I was being summoned to the principal's office. A tinge of rebellion and anger raced through me.

"Tony says we need to meet with them this morning; otherwise we'll have to wait until next week, and we'd both rather get this over with."

Teresa said she'd be with me in spirit. She told me I could do this. She told me this was important. "They probably just need to be sure you haven't gone crazy. They're just checking in."

I looked at myself in the mirror. I looked hard. *Maybe I have gone crazy.* Then I took a deep breath, and I looked gently. I met my eyes. *I'm on your side, sweet girl,* I told myself.

And then I felt God rising up within to meet me with words. "I'm on your side too, and I'm on their side. I don't play sides. I weave in and out of all of it."

But how can You be on their side? What if they are going to force me to go to church? What if Tony's going to lose his job over this? You told me not to go to church. I know You told me that. Sometimes I feel like the only thing that kept me out of the insane asylum was my decision to walk away from this whole Christianity thing for a time. I was so angry in church. How can I explain to them I was so angry? How can I make them see this was the only decision I could make?

The Divine rushed in in waves—waves of soothing, calming reminders that I have nothing to hide. I have done nothing wrong. I don't need to be defensive or angry about their desire to check up on me. I simply need to show up and answer their questions.

And then I felt as if I heard God say, "And you know, you can go back to church now. It's only been about four to five months, but you are changed. You are ready."

But I don't want to go back. Not ever. It's broken there.

"It feels broken here sometimes too," God said to me, touching my chest. "But you don't let that stop you."

My ego doesn't want to go back. My ego thinks going back means I've let them win.

Who's "them"? I wondered. *The Man? The Institution? Big Brother?*

My ego wants to prove a point. My ego wants to say, "Screw you, church; I've got God, and I'm doing it a different way." My ego is a bit vicious and catty.

I decided my ego and I would have to discuss later whether I'm ready to actually return to church. Why would I return? To keep my husband in good standing? To save face? To perform? To show myself I can enter in even with all my confusion and disagreements and still remain calm? To show myself that God can be on "their side" just as much as God can be on "my side"? To practice what it means to love unconditionally, to extend grace? I had to put my ego on hold so I could face the task at hand.

I picked up my phone and sent another text.

"I can do this," I told Teresa. "I have nothing to hide. I have no shame or regret. I did what I had to do to maintain my faith."

"Of course. You're not alone in this," she said, texting me whispers of encouragement as I left my kids with a babysitter and climbed into the car with Tony to make the short drive to the church offices.

"I'm nervous," I told him, "but I'm excited to do this. I feel like this is the next step, and God keeps reminding me I have nothing to hide."

I looked at Tony. He looked tired. Had I worn him down? Had I pushed him too hard? Was I going to cost him his job?

"Mandy, I want you to know that as much as I get frustrated with things at work sometimes, I do really trust these guys I work with. I know that they really do love and want the best for us. I think they see me struggling with finding my right fit on the team right now, and then to see you distancing yourself from church at the same time … it probably is just a bit disconcerting. I think, as our friends, they just sincerely want to check on us."

Tony was dead-on. That was exactly what the meeting consisted of. We met in a conference room across a long table, because it was the only private room available. Tony and I sat on one side, they on the other. The environment felt cold and impersonal, as if the principal and the vice principal were flexing their intimidation muscles to get what they wanted. I expected Donald Trump to walk in at any minute and break the news to Tony that he was fired.

However, the moment they began to talk, all coldness left the room. It was still awkward but no longer frigid and rigid and corporate. They *were* worried about me and Tony, about our marriage, about our family, about our health and happiness. I was both relieved and touched by their reaching out.

"We saw on your blog that you were taking some time alone to think. You mentioned going into the dark place to find yourself, and you suggested that people check on you every now and then to see if you're okay. Well, this is us asking, 'Are you okay?' Tell us where you're at," they said.

"Am I really in a room with three men who are giving me the opportunity to talk about how I feel? This *never* happens!" I said jokingly, and we all laughed a little nervously. This wasn't easy for any of us.

Tony was quiet the entire time. They had heard from him on several separate occasions about how he was doing, but he wanted to give them a chance to hear from me. I felt like our marriage was changing in this way, and it was strengthening our bond. We are now more attuned to each other's needs, giving each other space and independence as necessary.

So I talked, and I felt surprisingly calm. I felt like Tony trusted me and believed in my words. I was free to be myself, unashamed. No speaking to people-please. Just raw Mandy. This was major progress.

I told them everything in as few words as possible. About getting angry in church and feeling like God was telling me to take some time away. About not reading my Bible but finding God talking to me in other ways. About wanting to be an artist but not knowing if Christianity would extend to me that luxury. About wanting to believe in Jesus but having so many unanswerable questions. About why I left my small group and about how my relationship with God had never felt so rich. About being a mom and a wife and a good

Christian and losing Mandy in the midst of it. About feeling like a loner in church, like no one saw things the way I saw them. About feeling like God was more personal and mysterious than the church was letting Him be.

Then they talked some. Sharing their own personal stories of dark days of faith or failure to find their fit at a church. Sharing how they worked through that in their marriages. They told me they were proud of me for working through my mess with such passion and intensity.

"I think you have brilliant gifts inside of you, and we have yet to see all that God is going to do with your words and your art and your honesty," one of them said. "It's going to be fun to watch you in the years to come."

It brought tears to my eyes. My vulnerability was met with love. And even if they didn't agree with all my decisions, they did respect my need to do whatever was necessary to save myself and my relationship with God.

They asked Tony and me to consider whether we felt our fit was right at that church. They loved us, and they wanted us to stay, but they didn't want to force us to be there. More than anything, they just wanted us to feel like we belonged. That where we were was where we were meant to be. Where we wanted to be.

I felt angst dripping off of me and rolling away down the slick conference table never to be seen again. *This must be what it feels like to start to heal,* I thought.

I am currently walking very gingerly back into places as God leads. Two weeks ago I returned to church. It is not easy to be there, but God keeps talking me through it, in my mind and my heart. I take it a week at a time. I say, "Am I going back this week, God?" I say, "Do I have the grace to do this?" It helps me to know that I'm making the choice. That I'm not being forced to go.

I keep thinking about the quote in *The Shack* about freedom: "You will grow in the freedom to be inside and outside all kinds of systems and to move freely between and among them."[4]

I love, love, love this quote. I don't have to agree with everything that is being said and done at church in order to be at church, just as I don't have to agree with everything other people say and do in order to engage with other people. The Divine is filling me, making me bigger than my need to be right all the time or defend or explain myself. A little less ego, a lot more free spirit. A little less self, a lot more Self. Teresa and I have been referring to this as the Mona Lisa choice.

In the movie *Mona Lisa Smile*,[5] Julia Roberts' character is a freethinking art professor at a women's university in the fifties. She teaches the girls to question what tradition has taught them to be, to question the societal roles they must fill. Her presence on the conservative campus ruffles a few feathers, and she is told she can stay on as professor only if she follows certain rules. At the end of the movie, she has a decision to make: Will she stay or will she go?

I have always been proud of her for leaving. There is a part of me that wants to flip my middle finger at the university and say, "She doesn't need to limit herself and her voice by staying and living by your stupid rules." And while this is true, I'm realizing that there may be instances where staying and playing by the rules, albeit not agreeing with them, can allow access to the internal workings of a system that needs to be changed. If every freedom fighter left the fight saying, "I don't need this, because, damn it, I am free," then how would other prisoners ever find their own freedom?

Teresa teases me that I am quite good at beating people with my grace stick. I've learned what it feels like to experience a relationship with God that is full of grace and freedom, and I so long for everyone to have it that I'm willing to beat them into submission. It's such an oxymoron, but it's so difficult to put down the stick and gently lead people into grace.

I realize now that my birdcage is unlocked, and I'm free to fly, so when I look around with the veil removed from my eyes and see other Christians' cages open, I wonder why they aren't flying. "What are you waiting for?" I shake and rattle their cage, but I only manage to scare them all the more.

I realize that God is love, and in His infinite love, He allows people to stay in their cages when they are scared. He even allows them to bite at others who try to approach their cages. He gives them the choice.

Love means letting go of the need to be right and sitting with people where they are. To have the patience, like *The Little Prince*,[6] to sit a little closer to the fox every day until you can tame the fox enough to trust you. I haven't had the patience for taming anyone. Or maybe I am the wild one, with darting eyes and scurrying feet, my fur a bit ruffled and matted. Maybe I'm the wild one who thinks if I get close to the prince, then I'll lose some of my foxiness. And I'm really beginning to love my foxiness. Can I be the fox I was created to be and still be tame enough to sit close with people?

It would seem I'm damned if I do and damned if I don't. Unless ... unless I can realize that I am truly a changed person. Unless I can have an internal confidence that as I interact with Christianity and religion and people whom I used to perform for, I'm not who I once was. I am a cocreator with the Divine Artist, and He is making all things new.

I am new, and this pain I'm feeling as I forge new territory is different from the pain I used to experience when I was addicted to performance. This pain is simply the pain of walking into the unknown. Of entering into places and relationships without having to prove I am right. It's the pain of being messy, of doing things without the outcome in mind. Of being moved by the Spirit.

I am where I am in regard to church and Christianity because God has commissioned me to create something new for Him in a place that once meant something else to me. There is tension as the monsters of my past come rushing in, but He promises to be with me, soothing, healing, offering perfect love and complete comfort, a love that casts out all fear. A love I can trust, even when it has the appearance of the love I used to think I had to earn.

I am not selling out. I am returning as a freedom fighter who fights with the weapons of love and grace. And sometimes I'm learning that I really don't have to *fight* at all.

I wonder, *Can I walk on this narrow road with others without feeling crowded, without throwing elbows to make more space? Can I manage to trust, to be vulnerable, to have a little tamed edge to my wildness? Is there room here on this narrow road for others who perhaps don't do things like I need to do them? Do we all have to look the same to be on this road together?*

This is new territory, and I daily pray for the grace to love as I have been loved while simultaneously not questioning the love that flows freely for me. Today I believe in God, in His wild Spirit, in Jesus, who makes it all possible. I still have more questions than answers, but I have love and belonging and purpose, and that is enough. May what I believe today be enough to erase the doubts of yesterday and carry me through the doubts of tomorrow.

Chapter Fifteen

Labeled

I threw a whisk the other day. It was no small whisk either. It was one of those made from dense metal, twice as heavy as a typical whisk. It was a whisk I'd bought at a yard sale from a grandma who probably once used it to whack her children on the butt in between stirring her stew.

I was cleaning out the dishwasher midday, trying to prepare myself and the kitchen for taking on the task of making lunch. It had been a hard morning. I kept snapping at my kids for reasons unbeknownst to any of us. I just woke up in a fury, something I haven't done in a really long time. Perhaps it had to do with sleeping in and not having some time to myself before child number four crawled in bed with me demanding his "Mmmmm," otherwise known as breakfast.

I was slightly scared of the person I was that morning, because I reminded myself a lot of the Mandy I thought I wasn't anymore, and I'm not a big fan of backsliding.

I managed at some point in the morning to sneak some time alone in my bedroom while my kids were entertained in some exciting game of the imagination. I was reading a book called *Dark Night of the Soul*. Not exactly light and uplifting reading material. "Faith voids and darkens the understanding as to all its natural intelligence, and herein prepares it for union with Divine Wisdom," I read.[1] I was having trouble focusing, though, because I kept thinking about Jesus. I couldn't get Him out of my mind. *Why am I so ill at ease with Him right now?* I wondered.

I began to think through what I know of Him, and quite frankly, I couldn't find much wrong with Him. Much like Mary Poppins, He seemed "practically perfect in every way."[2] I didn't even hate Him for that. I felt a bit like Pilate, reluctant to condemn this man in whom I could find no fault.

I have friends who are spiritual but don't believe in Jesus. We have a lot in common when we talk about matters of faith. God seems to overarch everything, in all, through all. I wondered why God could not be enough. Why this man Jesus? And why am I ashamed of Him? Why do I hate this embarrassing label *Christian*?

As I walked downstairs, I could feel the darkness swallowing me up. Everywhere I turned, the things that were once light were now snuffed out. Blackness around every corner. I was stuck in my head, turning around in circles, demanding my brain to give the answers that used to make sense.

I was late in making lunch, but I still couldn't bring myself to start it. I had to get to the bottom of this ache I was feeling. The ache that was all too familiar lately. Madeleine L'Engle wrote in her book *Walking on Water*, "The faithfulness of doubt ... is a prerequisite for a living faith.... It is brave enough to ask questions, no matter how fearful."[3]

Tears stung my eyes, and I tried pinching them tight so the tears would go away. They were making my brain fuzzier, and I needed my brain.

I had flashbacks of the strong black woman who coached discus and shot put for the women's track team in high school. The whites of her eyes were big and bright next to the contrast of her dark skin, and she seemed a bit crazed one day as she playfully cornered me in the locker room and told me to stop crying.

"Strong women don't cry. We're athletes. We can't be weepy. You gotta be strong. We can't have this blubbering." She laughed big and bold, all the way from her gut. I felt puny, small, pathetic in her shadow. If I went to the left, she went to her right to block me. If I went to the right, she shifted her weight to her left to immobilize me. I wanted to head-butt her in the face. She was too close. Too close in proximity, but even more so, too close to the raw parts of me. Tears are vulnerable, and she was shaming me for each and every one.

A second, highly contrasting scene flashed into my mind. I was sitting in a small office, one tiny little room in the entirety of what makes up the campus of Focus on the Family in Colorado Springs. I was meeting with my professor, John Eldredge, and I was discussing with him some of the questions of my faith. I remember feeling confused, much like I was feeling right now standing in my kitchen staring down a full dishwasher.

"So many of the people I'm meeting here at Focus believe in predestination. They think God chooses some of us who He wants and some of us who He doesn't want. Is that true? I don't feel like that's true. But I've been told not to trust my feelings.

"I just want to know God loves me and that I have a choice in the matter whether or not I want to love Him back. I just want to stop feeling so confused about my faith so I can live that life to the full you keep talking about. I don't know what I believe anymore. I want so badly to know the God you talk about, who lives in story, who takes us on adventures, who battles through light and dark, who actually loves us, all of us, where we're at."

I wasn't making any sense. I was crying, tears dripping onto my skirt. I felt uncomfortable in my clothes, as though they were too tight and wrinkly. My face felt hot from embarrassment. Snot threatened to run down my face.

He handed me the tissue box.

"I'm sorry I'm crying. I can't seem to get my act together. I didn't mean to come here and blubber."

He looked at me, his eyes intense yet soft with empathy. To this day I would swear Jesus Himself was staring out at me from the shell of Eldredge's body. He was close too, just like my coach in high school. He was seeing me raw. I kept rubbing my eyes hard, willing my tear ducts to dry up, willing the hose to get a kink in it somewhere.

"Don't apologize for your tears," he said. "Don't ever apologize for your tears," he repeated with added fervor. "They reveal the feminine nature of God, a side that is soft, nurturing, deeply passionate, and caring. We need to see more of that side of God. Thank you for being brave enough to share it with me here today."

I will never forget his words. They were the light to the darkness of my locker rooms. They ushered in some soothing salve to a wound I didn't even realize existed. A feminine wound.

Perhaps tears don't get in the way of the brain. Perhaps the brain must be subservient to the tears. They will have to learn to get along. They will have to coexist. I will not have one bullying the other into a corner.

I opened the dishwasher and began emptying the clean dishes into their proper places in the cupboards and drawers. I was thankful that at least the dishes and silverware could be filed in a systematic order. Forks in the fork slot, spoons resting with the other spoons, knives pressed against other knives. Silverware made sense to me, but Jesus? I braced myself, holding on to the counter while leaning over the sink.

I believe in God. I believe in a wild Holy Spirit. I even believe in Jesus.

Why do I believe in Jesus? The Jesus who was God on earth. The Jesus who died unjustly. The Jesus who restores, redeems, repurposes my life. I don't know why I believe in Him!

I can't explain any of this to a single soul.

I can't explain it to myself. I believe in something I can't explain.

I felt as if Jesus were stalking me, breathing down my neck, asking, "What are you going to do with Me? Who do you say I am?" I stared blankly at the dishwasher and wondered if everyone has to deal with this God-haunt? I hope so. I don't want to be the only one. Who needs evangelism when God is a bounty hunter who tracks down our scent and won't leave us be until we give our answer? He was being ruthless.

It was at this point that my eyes landed upon the big metal whisk, still captive in the dishwasher silverware basket. I wrapped my hand around the cold metal and hoisted it out as if I were wielding a sword to face an enemy I couldn't name. With great anger I brought it back beside my ear and then thrust it forward, letting it fly through the air until it made a satisfying thud against the dining room wall and then clanked noisily on the floor before coming to a rest. Oh, dear, was I a mess. Cue the tears again.

As only fate can have it, this was the moment my husband walked in the door, home from his morning work at church and ready for lunch. The tears were still pouring down my face, and their pace only quickened when I saw him. He hugged me.

"What's wrong?" he asked.

Yet another dreaded question I didn't have a proper answer for. I tried to relax in his hug, glancing over his shoulder at the wounded whisk hiding in the shadows of the table. "It's me," I told him. "It's just me. I don't understand my faith anymore. I don't know why I believe in Jesus. Nothing makes sense." In the back of my mind I thought, *And I'm a pastor's wife. How's that for irony?*

"I'm sorry," he said, thankfully making no mention of the food that was supposed to be on the table. "I'd love to talk to you more about this."

"I'm sure a lot of people would," I spouted off, half-angry, half-dejected.

"Not to fix you," he said, a bit exasperated, sitting down in a chair. Then he added with regained patience, "Just to talk about it."

"I know, I know. Thank you," I said, finally finding some hidden reservoir of strength within me to begin lunch preparations.

My six-year-old daughter Charis walked into the kitchen. My back was to her. As I turned to face her, I noticed she had the whisk in her hand. "I found this on the floor, Mommy. It was underneath the table."

"That's because I threw it," I told her.

Her eyebrows immediately rose, and her lips quivered, as if she wondered if it might be okay to burst into a smile. I giggled despite myself, grateful for the release of positive energy.

"You threw it?" she asked, her face unapologetically happy now.

"Yes, I threw it. I was angry, so I threw it at the wall." I was laughing now, uncontrollably. The kind of laugh that usually only occurs late at night when you're slaphappy and have lost all restraint, but every now and then occurs after a good hard cry and a terribly confusing morning.

"Mommy threw this because she was angry," she said, laughing as she held up the heavy whisk, announcing my fantastic feat to her three siblings and her daddy.

"At least she didn't throw it at a kiddio. That thing would hurt," Tony replied. He was laughing too now, apparently thankful for a chance to ease the tension he had walked in on.

It was the laughter that gave me my answer. Not the answer to the Jesus question or the "Why do I have to believe in all this same Christian stuff if I'm a totally different person now?" question. In the laughter, I heard the heart of a child, and the heart of a child reminded me of a faith that is simple. To keep faith simple, you don't require answers. It's like Zoe says when her brother turns on behind-the-scenes footage from *Power Rangers*: "I don't want to watch this, because I want to believe in the magic still."

Christianity has felt so lame to me at times because it claims to know, to understand, to have a foolproof formula for a God who won't be held down by such a thing. It threatens to take away the magic.

I have spent years sorting out the Divine, systematically placing Him into the cupboards and silverware drawers of my life, memorizing verses that will convince others of the answers, which are provable because the Bible says they are. And now ... now I see that the answers cover only the territory I know about God, but there is much I don't know. In fact, I don't even know what I don't know.

Today my breath was taken away as I realized how little I was actually standing on. What if I want to believe simply because I believe. It all sounds so foolish, so childlike, but I don't have anything else to cling to. The whisk can attest to the anger I'm left with when I realize the ultimate answer to the majority of my questions of faith is, "I don't know."

Madeleine L'Engle wrote, "I asked questions ... and the ... theologians answered them all—and they were questions which should not have been answered in such a finite, laboratory-proof manner. I read their rigid answers and thought, sadly, 'If I have to believe all this limiting of God, then I cannot be a Christian.' And I wanted to be one."[4]

My friend Teresa says this another way: "The more you learn, the less together you will feel, *but* the more together in grace you will be." Grace excuses the things I don't understand and reminds me that I am complete anyway.

I am an artist. I live to be able to put expression to the mysteries we feel inside us, but I think it robs something of our own personal faith when we start marketing it door-to-door like an overeager and insecure salesman. Why would I try to pawn off my faith on someone else or try to package it up into some neat little box tied with a pretty bow when the depth of my faith has only transpired in the places I have allowed it to get the most messy?

I may be labeled as a Christian, but I'm in a love affair with a divine Being who knows no such labels, nor does He define me by them. I'm a spiritual seeker on a pilgrimage, a mystic vagabond, a ragamuffin soul, a messy canvas. Call me what you will; this love knows no bounds, nor does it require my answers. And I have the echoing sound of a clattering whisk and a child's giggles to remind me that it's okay.

When I was in college, I took my first-ever photography class. It was in the days before digital cameras, so purchasing rolls of black-and-white film with my limited college budget made me feel as if I was shooting with gold. I searched hard for every shot.

My roommate would drive me around off-campus, because I didn't have a car, and we would roam with no plan in mind until something caught my eye. "Stop. Pull over!" I would say, and I would throw open the car door and rush out into a field to get a picture of a dilapidated barn, or I'd step up onto a downtown curb on trick-or-treat night to catch a girl in her lopsided, yellow Teletubby costume.

One time we decided to go to a nearby park and see if anyone was milling around. We called the park the Covered-Bridge Park, because in the middle of the grounds, there was a covered bridge you could walk across. As we found a parking spot, I got excited because there was a handful of teenage boys out skateboarding. They were doing jumps out of the gazebo and onto the park sidewalks.

As my roommate and I approached them, they refused to make eye contact with us. They didn't seem interested in having us interrupt their skateboarding session, but I was thinking like an artist, and I was determined to get some precious shots on my expensive film.

"I'm taking a photography class at college, and we're doing a study on people, and I wanted to know if you'd let me take pictures of you guys."

They looked away from me and at each other. One of them smiled nervously, as if to say, "You're kidding, right?" A few of them, like the girl who was seated inside the gazebo, remained cold and straight-faced. I figured out which one of them was their leader by the way the others kept looking at him for his response. He had long sideburns and a goatee. His ears had thick, metallic hoop earrings, and he wore a thick chain necklace around his neck. Through his eyebrow ran a short rod, drawing attention to his attractive and intense eyes. His pants were big and baggy, making his lower torso look a bit like it was stuffed inside a trash bag, prepared, perhaps, for an invigorating potato-sack race.

I turned toward him and said, "I'm taking black-and-white photos, and I print them myself. If the photos turn out any good, I could make you a print and bring it back to you sometime. I bet you don't have many pictures of you skating."

He smiled, and his smile lit up his face. He looked rather shy. He looked at the girl in the gazebo, who, I would later find out, was his girlfriend. She took a drag on a cigarette and rolled her eyes and tossed her head away from him.

"Okay. You can take pictures," he said.

While I was taking photos, they really warmed up to us. A few more of their friends straggled in and wanted shots taken of them as well. Even the girlfriend let me photograph her. We had some decent conversation, talking about what school they went to, what music they listened to, and what they did for fun. The Covered-Bridge Kids, which is the name I affectionately began to call them, assured me they were in that park every evening. "We have nothing better to do," they said. So I promised to return someday with prints.

We returned one cold evening with a few of our friends and a small wad of cash. Our intention was to buy pizza and sit in the park and eat supper together at dusk. Sure enough, as we pulled up, a few of the Covered-Bridge Kids were there, and we knew more would trickle in as the night went on.

"I have prints," I said, walking up to the boy I now thought of as their leader. He smiled at me and reached for them. His girlfriend and a couple other guys leaned over his shoulder to look at them. "Cool," they said. "Oh, look. There's my cigarette, and we're holding hands," the girlfriend said vulnerably.

"We thought we'd buy you guys pizza tonight and eat supper with you if you're up for it." I felt as if I was inviting myself to their home. And I guess, in a way, I kind of was. Their eyes lit up.

While we waited for a couple of my friends to go pick up the pizzas, we somehow got involved in a wild game of Chinese freeze tag. We blew fog with our breath as we covered the park lawn with our antics. I went to dive through the legs of one boy dressed in black, so as to unfreeze him, when I heard the person who was It approaching behind me. He was sucking in big gasps of breath. "Maybe I should stop smoking," he said, laughing at himself as he doubled over, resting his hands on his knees.

I felt a rush in my veins. I still feel it to this day when I think of it. These tough Covered-Bridge Kids had dropped their protective hard outer shells to gallivant like grade-school kids in an innocent game of tag. I felt for one moment as if we were slipping into each other's worlds, unified by our humanity.

As we sat huddled together eating pizza that night in the gazebo, one of the guys said, "I'd love for a cop to come by tonight. They'd see you here, and they wouldn't know what to think."

"What do you mean?" one of my friends asked, puzzled.

"Well, the cops don't like us hanging out in this park. They say we make trouble. They say that people call and complain when we're here. That we vandalize the park. That we break things with our skateboards. One time we even got blamed for busting out the Christmas lightbulbs on the covered bridge."

"Well, did you?" I asked.

"Did we what?" he replied.

"Did you bust the lightbulbs?"

"No, it wasn't us."

I looked at him, raising my eyebrows so as to question him.

"I swear. I don't know who it was, but we didn't do it. We get blamed for everything. They want to padlock the gazebo so we can't be in it, but we have a right to be here just as much as anybody."

I think about the Covered-Bridge Kids as I type up this chapter on labels. I think about how easy it is to slap labels on things and claim that we know them. That we have them figured out. Teenagers dressed in black, wearing chains, smoking cigarettes, and hanging out in city parks after dusk are *hooligans*. The crashing sounds of their skateboards announce their destructive intentions to a world they can't seem to find their place in.

But hooting and hollering through one crisp winter night in a game of freeze tag made me wonder if the cops were missing something, because they've never hung out in the neighborhoods they patrol, taking only the upright citizen's word for it that these kids were a menace and needed to be removed.

Maybe I can be a Christian and yet not be what that label implies.

And maybe God can be something other than the Christian labels I have associated with Him. Isn't He the God of everything, of everyone? Maybe I need a crisp game of sucking wind between my cigarette drags to see that God is laughter in unexpected places. That God is in the messy grass stains that come from vulnerably diving in between a pair of worn, black sneakers. And that this is how we really begin the unfreezing process of our hearts in a lifelong game of freeze tag that we all must participate in.

Chapter Sixteen

Rhythms

There are weeks when living by faith is harder than other weeks. This is one such week for me.

My friend Paige wrote to me once, "No canvas is beautiful without the contrast, the tones of color, the ebb and flow, the perspective. These [dark] days give you the contrast to the days when you feel light, bursting with words and color and energy. These are all days that are part of you, your life, your family, your art. The whole. Today you captured the ebb.... And you will find the other side—the flow. Life is the balance—feel it all."

I wonder what it would be like to just let myself feel this. To feel it without guilt, without pressure, without the performance angst in me rising to rescue my God-forsaken life. To simply say, "I'm having a bad week," and to ride the waves of that bad week without flailing, because I know the flow will return. It always does. Like clockwork. Like nature. All things repeat.

Anne Morrow Lindbergh said in *Gift from the Sea*,

We have so little faith in the ebb and flow of life, of love, of relationships. We leap at the flow of the tide and resist in terror its ebb. We are afraid it will never return. We insist on permanency, on duration, on continuity.... The only real security is not in owning or possessing, not in demanding or expecting, not in hoping even ... but living in the present ... and accepting it as it is now.[1]

I think it is timely in my life to be facing another ebb. You see, just last week I started implementing some field research of my own life, suggested to me by Teresa, who writes for a blog titled *Right Brain Planner*.[2] I was finding myself falling into certain slumps and had no bearing for how often they were occurring, if certain events were leading up to these slumps, or if they were actually coming out of nowhere. I was also searching for a way to gracefully ride the waves of both the ebbs and the flows, taking advantage of the flows as they came and breathing through the ebbs that couldn't be avoided.

My performance mentality had never taken into account ebbs or flows—it was just gas pedal to the floor and try to avoid any head-on collisions. But I can see through this messy journey God has me on that I am in need of a new sort of rhythm to live by. A rhythm that fluctuates and gives grace. A rhythm that is able to adjust with the free-flowing and ever-shifting winds of the Spirit. If I have the Spirit living in me, then it only makes sense that I would learn to dance to the Spirit's rhythms rather than set my jaw in determination to live by my own prefabricated plan. It is an idea that fascinates me and that I am trying to implement with much anticipation and wavering faith.

For the longest time, I have associated negative feelings with evidence that I am not in God's will. If I'm tired, I must have pushed too hard using my own strength and not God's. If I'm angry, then I must have taken on my own cause instead of letting God be my defense. If my feelings got hurt, then I must be caring too much about what others think. If I'm sad and depressed, then I must not be looking to God for joy.

Christianity is supposed to be filled with joy and peace and love and contentment and energy, so it would make sense that I have felt a bit guilty whenever the opposite appeared in my life or the lives of others. I would rush in with my bag of tools to try and fix my life or the life of another. Offering Band-Aids that my religion had promised me would heal all, and then feeling discouraged when I knew the wound was still real and deep below the brown plastic sticker I had used to conceal it.

Now I'm considering feelings a different way. I'm considering them to be normal. The way we deal with messy lives as human beings is to expect a range of emotions. We should expect them out of ourselves, and we should expect them out of others. Emotions aren't always signs that something needs to be fixed; they are signs that we're alive, that we're breathing, that we're engaging in a world that is in motion. But there is a part of me (perhaps my soul?) that does not have to be carried off by these emotions. It's as if I am an open vessel and the emotions are just passing through. I see them; I document them with interest; I may even have to, from time to time, apologize for what actions they cause from me; but the vessel is free to stand back and watch them come and go while still remaining solid, complete, unharmed.

My faith in God is not dependent on these feelings that ebb and flow.

It's comforting to see myself as untouchable on the level of the soul. A place where I can gather myself even as the emotions want to convince me everything is pure chaos. Even as my body must go through the motions of screaming and then apologizing, of feeling pain and then resting, of raising my fists in self-defense and then admitting defeat. I have a soul that has been set free by grace and stands acquitted. A soul that can brilliantly ride whatever waves the Spirit asks of me. The ebbs *and* the flows.

It is different to ride the ebb if I know it couldn't be helped and it's normal. It is different to ride the ebb if I know the redeemed part of me is still intact. It is different to ride the ebb if I realize I'm not doing so because I have failed or sold out but because this is simply where the Spirit says I must go next. It is different to ride the ebb if I am tuned into the patterns of my life, aware of the vibrational changes, and know that the heaviness I'm feeling doesn't have to rule my responses. This is simply a shifting sea, and I can let it change because it is not the sea that grounds me. It is the Maker of the heavens Himself.

I'm attempting to look on things in this new light. To know that I am on a quest with the wildness of God living and moving inside of me. That I'm a coheir to the throne of the Divine, and that I move with a Spirit who is bigger than just me and my feelings. I move with a Spirit who is connected to the universal good, and universal good must always be about more than just me.

Sure, there are times when my negative emotions are warning signs that I haven't listened properly to this Spirit, and I have let myself become a victim yet again to people pleasing and performing and living out a religion that sucks the life out of me. There are times when my anger is cautioning me that I'm ready to grow, to move on, to reevaluate how I'm living and implement some changes. But there are other times when the negative emotions that rise up in me are simply part of living out what the Spirit is asking of me.

Negative emotions need not always alert me of wrongdoing. Sometimes they are just there and must be allowed the opportunity to pass by rather than take up residence. Sometimes they are a part of healing. Sometimes they are a part of learning. Sometimes they are just part of living this messy life. I am learning to listen to my body, evaluating my negative emotions instead of assuming they are always proof that I am in the wrong.

There is a much more fluid dance going on than I have ever allowed myself to be a part of. It sweeps back and forth across the floor in grandiose motion. It allows for twirling both in the ebbs *and* the flows of life. It's a dance that religion has never allowed me the permission to partake of.

John O'Donohue talks about these unforced rhythms in *Anam Cara*:

> When you lose rhythm, your life becomes wearingly deliberate or anonymously automatic. Rhythm is the secret key to balance and belonging. This will not collapse into false contentment or passivity. It is the rhythm of a dynamic equilibrium, a readiness of

spirit, a poise that is not self-centered.... When you are in rhythm with your nature, nothing destructive can touch you. Providence is at one with you; it minds you and brings you to your new horizons. To be spiritual is to be in rhythm.[3]

A couple of days ago, I was reading books with my kids. It was storming outside as all five of us climbed up onto the top bunk bed with a big stack of library books. We got situated with pillows behind our backs and blankets over our legs, and we watched the gray skies flash with lightning, and we listened to the rumble of thunder and the whish of wind as it slapped raindrops against the window and roof.

We read a book that day called *The Red Tree* by Shaun Tan.[4] The illustrations were breathtaking, and the author told the story of a little girl who believes she has lost all hope. On the final page of the story, the little girl returns to her room, where the book started, and she finds a little sprout of hope, characterized by a red leaf that is shooting up through her bedroom floor.

On our first reading, we were so taken by the story and by the dark loom of sadness that was threatening to swallow her that we didn't notice a little red leaf had been painted on every single page. But when we saw the leaf at the end, we had the hindsight to wonder if the red leaf had been there all along.

"Oh, my goodness, you guys," I said to my kids. "Do you suppose that red leaf was there all along, and we missed it?"

"Let's go back and look," one of them said.

Sure enough, on every single page, there was a little red leaf, hidden to the eye that is focused on the dark. But when you're looking for it, it easily comes into view.

"Do you guys ever feel like things are never going to get better?"

"Yes," my son Nehemiah spoke up, his face contorted into a look of regret and empathy. "Sometimes when I do something mean to hurt my brother or my sisters, I feel like such a bad boy. And I go to my room, and I sit, and I feel so ugly I just want to take a knife and put it in my chest. I want to die because I messed up so bad."

My kids are graphic this way. My daughter once, in a fit of rage, told me she was going to chop my head off. Later she laughed embarrassingly about it as she apologized, saying, "I'm sorry, Mommy. I would never do that. I only said it because I was angry."

It's easy for me to freak out when I hear my kids talk like this. What have I exposed them to that has made their minds so twisted and dark? But really I think it comes from active imaginations. And really I think I'm raising little artists who feel emotions on a level that is hyperintensive. So I try not to hear their words literally. I try to hear them like poetry. I try to hear the words as if my children are just really good at using them to express the waves of ebbs and flows that we know so well in humanity.

When my son said that about the knife and his chest, I at first wanted to make sure he knew I didn't want him using a knife in that way; that knives are meant for cutting up food at the dinner table or cutting through a piece of rope to create a lasso or, on occasion, protection. But I also wanted to hear the message behind his words. To help him unpack his gut reaction. To discuss that feeling of darkness that comes over us in a fit of shame. I wanted him to know the red leaf exists somewhere on the other side of that cloud of darkness.

"When you looked through the book the first time, buddy, did you see the red leaf on every page?"

"No," he said. "I was looking at other things. Like the big fish that was going to swallow the girl. Did you see the leaf?"

"No, I didn't. Not the first time. And when you're embarrassed or angry because you've gotten in a fight with your brother or sisters or even me, you don't notice the leaf either. But does that mean it isn't there?"

"No, I guess not. But I can't see it. I can't make myself feel happy then."

"Not then. But a part of you has to believe that leaf is there, that happiness is hiding. And you have to hold out for hope, hold out for the vision to see it."

I hope that all of us in my little family of six manage to always hold out for that hope, even if it just means sitting numb and staring off into space for a while first. It's not really something you can convince a person to do, though. I realize it has to come from an internal desire, an internal choice, an internal belief that there is something bigger that has your best interests in mind. How do you teach someone about that in-your-gut determination to hold out for more?

Last night I was talking to Tony after a discouraging bike race he competed in. He was feeling really down, and I said to him, "I just don't want you to quit racing."

Besides being a pastor, Tony has made great strides in his cycling accomplishments, going from out of shape and riding on a borrowed mountain bike in sweatpants and tennis shoes to actually placing in several races on his own legit road bike. He has blogged about this journey on JoetoProCycling.com. He has fought hard for his health and for his passion, and it has greatly fed into his overall quality of life. I don't want him to lose that. I don't want *us* to lose that. When you find something that brings you to life, it changes you. Tony is a changed man, and given the choice, I'd rather not revert to the days of before.

He sighed deeply and then responded to me. "When I talk like this, being frustrated with my races and with myself, people always assume it means I'm going to give up or that I'm being too hard on myself. It's really hard to be transparent and honest when everybody is looking at you and expecting you to have the answers. But I don't have the answers. And tonight I'm embarrassed by my performance, and I just don't want to write about it."

"Boy, do I understand that," I said to him. "But you know this is exactly why you have to write about it."

"Yeah, I know. This just sucks. But I'm not going to quit. No way am I getting off my bike."

I am married to someone with the determination to hold out for red leaves sprouting through bedroom floorboards. I hope my son Nehemiah can get that same determination through my husband's genes.

There is a way to walk and work in this life that isn't heavy or forced. There is a way to experience this present darkness and know it isn't so heavy that it will swallow me for good. There is a way to watch the anger and the disappointments and the sadness pass before me and know that it is but for a time, and that I'm twirling to rhythms I don't have to understand, so long as I can trust His music. The garden of my soul looks, especially this week, as if it might be overtaken with weeds, and yet I have no energy to uproot them. I watch them spring up among the beauty, and each one makes my breath quicken, stirring the performer in me to take action, but for some reason, I hear Him telling me to slow my breath and wait on His timing. And I have to trust that I really don't have the energy to take action right now, and that He won't let the weeds swallow the beauty.

"It's all such a mess. I am a mess!" I yell at Him.

I'm reminded of a little catchphrase that Teresa and I throw around. Whenever I feel like I'm stumbling in the dark, she'll say to me, "Here, I'm passing you the glitter glasses. Put them on." When she sends me a text, the glitter glasses look something like this: 8-) They're like night-vision goggles, allowing things to glow that I wouldn't normally see. They aren't Pollyanna glasses, because the lenses aren't rose-colored at all. With night-vision goggles, it's quite evident that it is still, in fact, dark. Very dark. But suddenly red leaves are illuminated with a neon-green glow, and I know there is something worth holding out for. Even in the darkness, even in the ebbs, there are gifts.

I remember when Teresa invited me to draw a circle in my journal. I still flip back and look at that page sometimes. I traced a Starbucks cup lid to give me a perfect circle, and along its circumference I wrote the words *My Bubble*. She told me to realize that no matter what comes at me, no matter the waves that threaten to drown me, it's as if I'm traveling in this tiny bubble, buffered by padding and insolation so that when I bump, it doesn't hurt me, at least not deeply, not where it counts. My substance remains intact. Nothing can completely destroy me. Not even poised little-boy knives that threaten my deeply heaving chest.

I feel better having written this. Processing God's grace and my humanity always makes me feel a little softer around my ever-hardening edges. I am not confined to the edges of a maze where Christianity is defined by ninety-degree angles and the definitive yeses and nos of harsh black lines. I am on a journey of grace where I swirl in a dance in the arms of my Beloved, who takes me places I thought I should never be and shows me that in His arms I am safe even here. At times we swirl so fast I bury my face in His chest and drink in the deep cologne of His beauty, intoxicated into restfulness. At other times I raise my head elegantly and take in the panoramic views that make my toes feel tingly beneath me. At still other times, I feel as if He is letting me lead, and I take us to places I thought He'd never go with me.

But the dance never ends. Though we travel periodically into the halls of the religious maze I used to live in, He shows me how, even there, lines can be danced over and darkness can be flushed with the light His presence brings. Though He allows me to dip back into the shadows of the valley of death, He does it only to allow me the practice of deep breathing and the inner release of my tension. I learn to breathe and trust, even there. Just as my muscles have found a deeper place for my yoga to take me, so my faith is finding a deeper place for my dance with the Beloved to take me. A place I could never have forced my muscles to go. A place that only comes in a posture of surrender. A posture of though I am great, yet am I small. The God who convinced me to listen to my deepest desires to be an artist and follow my heart is now convincing me to dance with Him even into the shadows of negative emotions.

I have to be completely honest. This has been the hardest chapter of the book to write so far. Not for lack of words. The words are flowing perfectly. But it's the timing that is messy. Typically I write when my kids are asleep. I wake early so I have time to pound the keyboard prior to interruptions. This morning was no different. I woke early, but the words didn't start coming until about seven, right at the time when my husband was ready to talk to me and my kids wanted their breakfast.

I have constructed the paragraphs of this chapter in between pauses where I have demanded silence and pleaded with little ones to get their own breakfasts. I have yelled in anger as I broke up petty arguments between my children, and I even made a mad dash to the curb outside when I heard the trash truck and remembered I had forgotten to take our trash out. It's ironic how parallel these words and my messy living have been this morning. Anger even in the midst of the obedience to write. Franticness even in the midst of creativity. He is doing this on purpose, of course, for me to see and give testimony to the stark blacks and whites of life that coexist, and the messy gray that ensues. This is the dance. I am twirling even now. And there are little bits of shrapnel I will have to clean up and weeds I will have to pluck when He leads me in the dance to do so.

Today may I live the words I'm writing and walk away from this piece without guilt or condemnation. May I make apologies as needed to my kids and husband but not make less of the flow of the words that managed to pour out despite the ebb of negative emotions that I am living in today.

Maybe my kids needed to know there are new things they can do for themselves that they had thought only Mommy could do for them. Maybe I needed to hear my husband say, in validation of my creativity, "Oh, I'm sorry. I just realized you're writing, and I'm interrupting." Maybe I simply needed to see the clear example of positive in the midst of negative. All I know is that today I danced to unforced rhythms, and I danced despite an overwhelming desire to be swallowed up by an ever-increasing darkness. These enlightening moments are what a romance is all about, and He has wooed me further in spite of myself. How can I love Him even for the ebbs? It is yet another question I may never have words to answer.

Chapter Seventeen

Conversations

In the course of writing this book, I have had some very honest and raw conversations with a handful of people. Conversations about spirituality seem to strip all the pretense and masks and protective walls away. It can be a rattling thing to realize what you thought you had figured out about yourself is really not you at all. Deeper down there are questions you often avoid while living a life that is busy and wearyingly strategized.

Being a Christian, I've engaged in several spiritual conversations throughout my life. I can remember discussing the book *Conversations with God* with the coworker who recommended it to me. I remember thinking if I could just read it and understand where she was coming from, then maybe I could help her see where she was wrong in her theology. My motive was always to win others over to my way of thinking, and I really thought I was doing it out of a love for them. I mean, I wouldn't want them to go to hell, right?

Sometimes I wonder, though, if I was doing it out of my own insecurity. Thinking, *If I could just prove to you that I'm right, then I wouldn't have to walk around with all these doubts. If I could get you to agree on Jesus and sin and salvation, then I could feel much more comfortable in my own wavering faith.*

This brings to mind a short exchange between two brothers in the movie *Signs*. One brother thinks miracles are possible and that there are no coincidences. Someone is orchestrating life so that it has meaning and purpose. He asks Mel Gibson's character, Rev. Graham Hess, what type of man he is, secretly hoping that they will be in agreement. Graham asks him, "Do you feel comforted?"

"Yes," the brother replies.

"Then what does it matter?" Graham answers rather matter-of-factly.[1]

The brother's countenance drops. You can tell he's shaken.

If I know what I believe, and it makes me feel comforted, then why am I so disturbed when others don't believe it along with me? Why does it shake me and make me feel like I need to go into some memorized persuasive salesman spiel?

Those conversations, like the one I had with my coworker about the book, were always hard. My knees would be wobbly and my palms sweaty. I would feel as if I was there on God's behalf, His acting attorney, and if I couldn't plainly represent His case and win the jury over, another soul would be lost for eternity. Afterward, I would rehash in my mind how the conversation went. Relive the feeling of my heart beating loudly in my chest, gathering pace as the jury seemed unimpressed and unmoved by my eloquent speeches salted with Romans Road Scriptures. I would soothe my wounded pride from the "unwon battles" by telling myself, "You did the best you could. It's the Holy Spirit's job to convict the heart, not ours." But part of me always felt sick. Sick because I knew my friendship with that person could never really be the same again, and sick because I wasn't sure who I was trying to convince more—the jury or myself.

But lately ... lately the conversations have been different. They've been different because I'm not having conversations to win anyone over. I'm having conversations because I'm the one asking questions. I can't tell you how freeing this is. For once I don't have to march "onward Christian solider" as if I'm off to war. I can march as a spiritual seeker who wants to have an authentic conversation about how we as humans interact with a Higher Being. Or, actually, I don't have to do much marching at all.

I listen to my friends who could be labeled as non-Christians talk about their spiritual lives, and I'm blown away by the encouragement they have to offer me. They seem to sprinkle fresh rain on this dry clay that is my body. I hadn't even realized parts of me were still cracking or brittle until the soft drops of water began to fall. I'm so tired I don't even reach for my Christian umbrella anymore. I just put my head up and soak in every drop I can find, because God is God and I know the things they are saying are true about Him even if they don't say it in Christianese. In fact, in some ways, He seems bigger to me when they talk, because He doesn't exist in the confines of what I can understand, control, or teach in a six-week Bible study.

It seems to me in these sorts of unforced conversations, I'm not trying to get my friends to move from point A to point B so that they can graduate from lost to unlost.

I recently got into a great discussion with some of my neighbors. They said they are Christians who hesitate to call themselves such, because they claim to have "fallen away." I asked them, "What have you fallen away from?" Because certainly God is everywhere, and falling away from Him is like saying, "I've fallen away from air and can't find it to breathe." They bring up things like church and reading the Bible and praying. I realize what they mean is they have fallen away from the rules, and since the rules have been taught as the only way you can commune with God, they have assumed He is no longer close by.

They mention their parents' strong faith, and that they consult their parents if they have questions about spirituality. I'm glad they have an honest relationship with their parents, but I wish they didn't feel so unworthy to talk to God or explore spirituality themselves. I think religion does this. It tricks us into thinking there is a long laundry list we must work through before we can approach God. I have felt that at times myself. If I could just get my religious life in order, then I could hear from God clearly. I have a hard time believing He might love me exactly where I am or be interested in the life I want to live. I falsely think that choosing Him must mean giving up everything I enjoy, everything I'm going after, everything I love. I follow a religion where it seems I must place sacrifice and penance on the list way before falling in love with God, so I never make it to the loving part of the relationship at all.

These conversations have been so helpful to me. Rich, deep, contemplative. They make me feel connected to people. That's what spirituality does for us. It gives us connection, meaning, a place to belong. It gives us spiritual context, an outlet for dealing with the big joys and the deep sorrows of our lives and trying to make sense of where we fit in all of that. Spirituality is a mix of internal and external. It's actually an attempt to try to merge the two—body and soul, what is seen and unseen. And sometimes, as my friends reminded me, the most ordinary of actions—hiking in the mountains, playing with puppies, spending time with a significant other, laughing, making dinner with family or friends—often bring a richness as deep and fulfilling as any spiritual conversation could bring. Living life at a slower pace so we might pay attention to the details and see the things and people around us as fragile rather than expendable. These are things that feed the soul and make us desire to give gratitude to some sort of Higher Being. Certainly there is someone to thank for this richness to life. And on the other hand, surely there is someone to comfort us when things take a turn for the worse. Or, in some cases, someone to yell at when the pain gets to be too much.

In all faiths, we're asking a lot of the same big questions. In fact, even those of us who call ourselves agnostic or atheistic, still have our humanity in common, and as humans we can relate on so many levels. I wrote a post on my blog called "I'm Tired of Being a Christian."[2] I enjoyed reading other people's thoughts about it. One woman mentioned over Twitter that she was an atheist, yet felt she could still relate to my post. I sent her a message saying we are probably more alike than either of our "sects" would be willing to admit. She agreed.

I think there is great value in finding the areas we do have in common. It's tough because we're constantly categorizing and shifting ourselves into groups. The haves and the have-nots. The people with "white" skin and those with different "colored" skin.

The Christians and the non-Christians. The men and the women. The religious and the nonreligious. The sinners and the saints. The liberals and the conservatives. The fat and the skinny. The athletes and the bookworms. The preps and the hoods. The straights and the gays. The young and the old. The rebellious and the rule followers.

The categorizing is as old as humanity itself. We do it without even clearly thinking about it. It is how we size each other up. It's our scientific investigation to make sense of our species. It's also our attempt to understand ourselves. We're conducting a search to belong, fulfilling our desire to hang our hat on some semblance of a tribe. "If I hang with these people, then I know who I am, and man, do I need to know who I am." "If I'm in this group, I know my marching orders, and man, do I need to know my marching orders." It also makes for a world of walls. As Robert Frost wrote, "Something there is that doesn't love a wall, / that wants it down."[3]

I'm kind of tired of the walls myself. I feel weary of doing all this mending to keep myself protected, and from what? From other humans who are just doing their best to figure out what is what in this life? I'm relieved to have a few conversations with friends through holes we've managed to find in the walls of our spiritual beliefs. Conversations that lift me up to see over the walls. That make me realize perhaps God is bigger than the walls I have lived behind and mended all these years. We don't have to solve anything or convince each other; we just have to talk, touch base, and say, "I'm okay. Are you okay? Are we both going to be okay?"

I'm excited to feel that I am coming to a place in my relationship with God where He directs my paths in ways that both protect me and pour me out into community. I don't have to feel as though

I must protect myself or defend my religion, because I'm learning to trust where He has me and where He guides me. When I am in conversation with other human beings, and the quickening panic rises in my chest, and I feel those haunted feelings and the questions that taunt me, saying, "What if I don't have answers for them?" or, "What if I can't defend what I believe?" or "What if I don't agree with them?" I remember that He is present with both parties.

I must remember I don't live in such a way to convince others. I live in such a way to be convinced myself. I don't have to prove this convincing to others, nor do I have to panic that they might not get me. I don't have to race to place rock on top of rock as quickly as possible so that the wall can hide me from their piercing eyes. Rather, I meet them eye to eye through the one hole in the wall, and I see if it is possible for us to connect on some level of our humanity and also our divinity. I hope that in me they might see that spark of the Divine and that in them I might see the same.

I was reading in *Eat, Pray, Love* about something the Dalai Lama said about his students. "They needn't become Tibetan Buddhists in order to be his pupils," reports Elizabeth Gilbert. "He welcomes them to take whatever ideas they like out of Tibetan Buddhism and integrate these ideas into their own religious practices. Even in the most unlikely and conservative of places, you can sometimes find this glimmering idea that God might be bigger than our limited religious doctrines have taught us."[4]

She goes on to say, "Doesn't that make sense? That the Infinite would be, indeed … infinite? That even the most holy amongst us would only be able to see scattered pieces of the eternal picture at any given time? And that maybe if we could collect those pieces and compare them, a story about God would begin to emerge that resembles and includes everyone. And isn't our individual longing for transcendence all just part of this larger human search for divinity. Don't we each have the right to not stop seeking until we get as close to the Source of wonder as possible?"[5]

I've always assumed that to find truth in someone who has different spiritual beliefs than I was to in some way take away from the truth I believe in. It was as if I was saying, "Because I can relate to what you're saying, and it actually even gives me great clarity and direction, I must therefore be condoning and desiring your entire way of life. I must be stating I would like to be you." And since I do not, in fact, want to be anyone else—I simply want to be myself—I have always felt it necessary that I point out other people's flawed beliefs so they know I'm agreeing with one small thing they've said, not choosing to become like them. It's a battle of my ego. My pride must speak up so that I'm not brought down to their level. This has been the way of Christian evangelism for me for quite some time.

And now … well, now I'm tired of muddying up relationships by always needing to have the last word and feeling sick about how the last word must have sounded. Now I'm not interested in someone else seeing me as right or knowing that I don't agree with their choices. Now I am so passionately in love with the Divine that I'm eager to find Him everywhere, in everything.

Let me learn from you, humanity. Let me take what you have to offer. Let me meet you eye to eye in the one place a chink is missing from our walls. Let me love you there and ignore the rest of the cold stone that is laid out between us, because I see a unique aspect of God in you, and I need all of God that I can find. I will love you not because you need me to love you or because I need to be loved back. I will love you because you are bigger than yourself. I will love you because you show an aspect of God to me.

I once met a man in the park when I was on a walk with my kids. His name was Gray Wolf Magic Dancer. At least that's the name his mama gave him when she left her teepee shortly after giving birth to him, and her eyes landed on a gray wolf and the tribal mountain dancers in the distance. His father, a white man, named him Mark. It's what his birth certificate reads, but he has resented that name ever since. "Just because you call a watermelon a peach," he told me, "doesn't mean it's a peach."

My daughter Charis was attempting to fill up her water bottle at the park, only to find that the water fountain was spraying water everywhere, making it nearly impossible to catch anything but a few drops in the bottle. Enter Gray Wolf, who kindly offered to show her his water-fountain-taming tricks. I could tell she was a bit nervous as she ran over to me asking, "Should I let him help me?" I nodded and told her I thought it would be okay.

Charis walked shyly over to him again, jumping back with big eyes when his dog, which was actually a wolf, stirred a bit under the picnic bench that she was chained to. I stood from a distance and watched the timid interactions between this man of the streets and my little blonde beauty. He managed to successfully fill the bottle and handed it to her with a smile. I was touched by his moment of generosity. We needed water, and he met our need. It was humbling.

I think you tend to take in the most details of a person when it's your first encounter with them. You notice things like interesting mustaches, crooked teeth, and a wheelchair full of simple belongings.

You also walk a fine line of "Can I trust you?" and "Can I get to know you?" Gray Wolf and I were testing each other out, dancing that awkward dance of a first meeting. But as I looked into his eyes, I could have sworn I had met him before. He reminded me of other people I have met along the way. People who are night and day different from me, who are watermelons while I am a peach. And yet who, just like me, simply long for the chance to be heard, the chance to talk, the chance to tell their story.

So we listened. We listened, my kids and I, as he taught us about shrieking cicadas and gray wolves and how to grow corn in sand. We listened as he taught us about reflecting light and homeless people and the Apache temper. We listened as he opened up doors to a world we have never been a part of, but one in which he was so graciously inviting us into.

At some point I realized my kids had all wandered off to play, and I thanked Gray Wolf for his time. He asked if I wanted to hear a sermon. "I'm a preacher too," he told me. Intrigued by this preacher who was lighting a cigarette and who told me he wanted to start a street ministry, I asked for his one-minute sermon.

"If I had one minute, I would give you my testimony. I would tell you about how I found Jesus in jail, and how my life has been forever changed. I would tell you about how I got myself a good family, good friends, a good church, and how I've been lining up some honest jobs I could do, even if I haven't decided to do any of them yet. I would tell you how it's possible to live just as richly as all these people who drive around in these nice, expensive cars," he said, motioning toward the street, "and to even be more content than most of them, all because of how Jesus changed me." He took a long drag on his cigarette and gave a crooked smile, nodding his head in satisfaction. The deer on his camouflage ball cap bobbed up and down with approval.

I'm not sure what it is about moments like these that leave me feeling hopeful inside, but as I walked away, I had this sense of connecting with humanity on a deeper level. Of seeing God and feeling His love, somehow, in the squinty eyes and suntanned face of Mr. Gray Wolf. I liked what I saw.

I believe there is a supernatural agenda of love that wants to envelop us if we could just manage to get out of the way for a split second and let Him have His way with us. Of course, to live like this, I must trust God first and foremost. Notice I said trust God first, not people, because people have been known to jab spears and shoot arrows through the holes in the walls instead of meeting me eye to eye. People are difficult to love. But actually, come to think of it, God can be too. He is wild and unafraid to let things get messy for the greater good. Which is why I am *choosing* to trust Him, even if He infuriates me. It is why a *personal* relationship with the Divine is so important. I need to know Him for myself. To see His hand work good in my life. To trust Him, I must love Him and believe He loves me in return.

And on the days when I can't, I reach out an arm to my fellow humans through the stone wall. I feel around until I feel flesh. I don't care if it's Christian flesh or not; I'm desperate here. I'm vulnerable. I say, "Excuse me. I'm gonna need some help. I'm feeling a bit jaded and alone. By chance, have you ever felt this way? By chance, do you have some hidden spring of divinity within you that I might take a sip from? I'm parched." And I don't give up until someone, somewhere through that wall is willing to offer me something life-giving in return. This is the business of loving, and there is cause for great celebration in the body of humanity when we remove one more stone from the wall.

Many times I have put up walls that even God Himself won't break through. I have to let Him in. I have to pay attention to where He's knocking. I might have to quit my "religion" for a while or do something crazy, like notice sunsets, chocolates, spring breezes, and brilliant songs. This sort of spiritual *magic*, for lack of a better term, requires a little imagination, a little determination, a little digging past the surface of "there is nothing here to see." I might have to let the Divine woo me with the things that uniquely stir my heart, even if they don't seem religious or proper. Like it or not, it's a romance, a dance that is perfected over time. There is risk, the letting down of one's guard, the messiness of unmet expectations and heated fights with brilliant making up to do afterward. It is full of high highs and low lows. Dark and light. Crescendos and decrescendos. And today I feel like I'm loving every second of it.

Oh, Lover of mine, where, where
will you show up next?
I hang on Your every word and color.
I await evidence of Your next
breath against my cheek.
I delight in the depth of Your mystery.
I love that Your artistic heartbeat attempts
to penetrate every human chest,

setting up hidden internal kingdoms
that we might all be royalty,
exploding Your light into the darkest
caves and valleys of all Creation.
Where will we find You
when we put down our idols
and marching orders
and peek through chinks
in ancient walls,
linking arms
as only Love can do?
You mean to tell me You are even here?
Oh, thank God. Thank God!

Chapter Eighteen

Truth

A good artist tells you the truth. Their truth. The truth as they see it, because for them that is the only truth that is real. I'm not always a good artist.

Writing a book about faith is dangerous for me. I have been inundated in the culture of my Christian faith for so long that it's easy to slip into answer mode. Let me regurgitate the truths I know should be true, so you'll like me or you'll know I've not fallen off the deep end, or you'll know those right answers actually work. It's easy to go into "I must defend the faith I stand on" mode; otherwise why do I believe it? I have this sinking feeling that if I admit to the days when none of it makes sense to me, or the days I want to say good-bye to the church and all its drama, or the days when I want to hide under a rock and cry because God seems a little too quiet, then I discount the good days when I really do believe in all of it.

I was thinking about the word *hypocrite*. This is really what I fear when I'm seeking truthfulness for my own life. When I stand looking at myself naked in the mirror, I just want to know I'm not fooling myself, I'm not pretending to have beliefs and opinions and feelings and characteristics and standards that I don't really have. I am not being hypocritical if I fail to believe today what I believed yesterday. I am being hypocritical if I fail to admit today that what I believed yesterday doesn't really seem all that possible anymore. In other words, I am not a hypocrite for being someone different today than I was yesterday. I am a hypocrite if I say I am the same today when I know full well I'm not.

I get nervous with my shifting truths. I constantly glance nervously over my shoulder, wondering if someone will call me out. "Aren't you the girl who said you loved Jesus just yesterday, and now you're throwing a whisk across the room because you don't know why you believe in Him?" I fear accusing eyes and raised eyebrows, shaking heads and disappointed shrugs. I fear truth must be one consistent choice, and if it deviates today from what I knew it was yesterday, then it makes the Mandy of today a liar. I don't want to be a liar.

The other night we had some of our friends over for dinner. These were relatively new friends we met through Tony's cycling, whom we're really enjoying getting to know better. At one point, conversation turned to the topic of tattoos, as I noticed a Greek inscription on the right arm of Holly, who was seated next to me.

"What does your tattoo mean?" I said in between bites of chocolate cheesecake and sips of a smooth red wine.

"It's Greek for 'know thyself.' Ralph Waldo Emerson has a poem called 'Know Thyself,' and it's an inscription on the temple at Delphi. The idea is that when you get to know yourself, you get to know the gods, or God, better." She lightly rubbed her hand over her arm as she explained.

"Wow. That's really cool. It sounds exactly what I'm learning in my own faith right now. Because I kind of went through a time when I lost myself. I didn't know who I was anymore, only who I thought I was supposed to be. And it's only been lately, as I've spent some time getting better acquainted with me again, that I have come to know God on an entirely different level."

We chatted a bit more about how sometimes in the Christian church, focusing on yourself is seen as selfish and even prideful. How I feel like sacrifice must come first, and yet sacrifice has sucked me dry.

"I bet you feel that even more as a mom of four kids," she said, "because you are constantly giving so much of yourself away."

I glanced over at my kids, who were sitting in the living room watching a movie with Holly's little two-year-old son, and I nodded in agreement.

"Yes, the mom thing certainly adds into that. It's much harder than I thought it would be." The overwhelming feelings washed over me again, like an ocean wave, pulling my feet with the undertow. For an instant I was envious of the other couple sitting at our dinner table who were in their mid- to late twenties and had no kids to speak of yet. I was so busy those years before Tony and I had kids. I was so busy being religious. Wasn't I? Did I even enjoy myself? I sure wish I could be who I am now and go back to those days of young married freedom. But the grass is always greener, and freedom is always a choice.

Maybe I'm too confused to be a parent. Maybe I should have thought about the commitment more before diving in so fully. I took in the behind-the-scenes view, the stair step of the backs of my kids' heads as they watched their movie, and my heart flooded with love. I'm full with affection for them, but I am so void of answers. I have no desire to be the strong one anymore. I'd much rather wiggle in between them on the couch and be another kid. But the couch is full. Where do I belong?

I asked Holly if she had any other tattoos, and at this point the other people at the table became a part of our conversation. Everyone started to share a bit about the tattoos they had and when they first got them.

"I don't think I want to get one, but I love hearing about yours," I said across the table to the couple sans kids.

"Why would you not want to get a tattoo?" Brandon asked me—Brandon whose legs are covered in tattoos that tell the story of his life.

"Well, I just don't think I could make a commitment. I have changed so much from who I used to be, and I figure I'll change a lot more. So anything I would get now probably wouldn't make much sense in the future. I can't commit to one thing I would want on my body forever."

He took a sip of his beer and ran one hand through his long beard. Then he leaned forward and said, "A tattoo isn't forever 'cause you don't live forever. You're thinking too far ahead. A tattoo is a statement about where you are today, and in the future, you'll see how where you were has gotten you to who you are now."

"Wow, that was really deep," someone at the table said, and we all laughed. But we knew it was true. We knew he was right.

I thought about his words. I'm not contradicting myself if my truth today is different from my truth tomorrow. That doesn't make me a hypocrite. I'm just sharing my journey. I'm putting a milestone down in ink, saying, "On this leg of the narrow road, I was in this place in my life. I will never forget this place."

Brandon's wife, Lindsey, interjected into the conversation, "We are all constantly changing anyway, right? I mean, I'm not the same person I was when I walked in through your front door a couple hours ago."

"You're right," Holly added. "Each of us has said something tonight that has changed another person in some way. And we'll walk away from this dinner tonight different."

"Right, exactly," Lindsey continued. "We're always changing."

Isn't that the truth? I thought.

Being an artist, I tend to make a lot of theories. It is painfully difficult to write about one such theory today with great passion and confidence, only to find that tomorrow that theory falls flat. With disappointment and dread I attempt to reach back into yesterday to say, "I didn't really mean that," but unfortunately, yesterday is already frozen in time, and I get no do-overs. I feel flat, paper-thin. That's what it feels like to be squashed daily and to start again. A clean slate.

I feel as if the me of today is being recklessly dishonest to the me of yesterday, and yet I can't figure out how to make it up to her. Today I just don't agree with yesterday's bold statements, and it makes me leery to make any sort of bold statement today for fear the me of tomorrow will prove it all bunk. I sit there with my head in my hands and wonder if I should just pretend today like the me of yesterday was in fact right. Perhaps that would make it up to her. But I know it's a lie. It's painful, this process of being true to oneself, of knowing oneself. In any given moment, an incredible portion of humility may be required to be true to the new feelings that are washing over me. It's where the artist begins to feel a bit mad.

Natalie Goldberg would agree with my friends Lindsey and Brandon. In her book *Writing Down the Bones*, Natalie says, "We think our words are permanent and solid and stamp us forever. That's not true. We write in the moment.... Watch yourself. Every minute we change. It is a great opportunity. At any point, we can step out of our frozen selves and our ideas and begin fresh."[1]

If you must know me, then you must know me one moment at a time. My husband lives with this weebling and wobbling sort of truth from me day in and day out. He handles it with much grace and patience. Yesterday he walked into our home dripping sweat from just completing a three-hour cycling ride. I didn't say to him, "Hello." I didn't say to him, "How was your ride?" No, I looked him in the eyes and said what was on my mind: "I think I'm okay with Jesus again."

He smiled. He is used to these random outbursts of spiritual conversation, especially as of late. He understands me and isn't surprised by it.

"He's a good guy," he replied, reaching around me for a piece of fruit.

I laughed nervously. I couldn't explain my sudden shift in beliefs. I couldn't even be sure I would like Jesus tomorrow. I relaxed. This is my husband, and he isn't going to ask me for my dissertation on my sudden newfound love for this holy man. Nor is he going to lord this moment of truth over me when my beliefs all come crashing down around my feet in a big heap, as they seem to be doing lately. Tony knew this was a truth for the moment, and he was okay with that, probably more than I was.

"I'm okay following Jesus if I have the free choice to, but as soon as you tell me I have to follow Him, or if I do follow Him, my life has to look a certain way, I'm out. I want no part. I'm far more rebellious than I ever realized."

"Jesus was a rebel too," Tony said, reaching past me again for a glass to get some water.

"I know. I think that's why I like Him."

Today being a rebel means that I don't have to be ashamed of the feelings I'm having on days when metal whisks go flying or flour goes up in a cloud of anger while making homemade noodles. I don't have to be ashamed of my truth. My truth is anger and fear and doubt. My truth is I am at the end of my rope, and I need help. My truth is what I believe about God isn't working for me today. My truth is this is all far more complicated and messy than I ever want to admit. My truth is I have no business being a mom to four kids who are looking to me for the answers. My truth is my God doesn't save me from sadness, fatigue, burn out, or anger. My truth is some days I wish He would, and I'm mad at Him when my life doesn't look perfect. My truth is all I want to do some days is sit on cafeteria walls, swinging my feet like a little kid and wearing a shirt that screams "Beware of God!" My truth is I am human just like my non-Christian friends are human, and damn it, if I didn't think I was better than them for figuring something out about this faith thing. My truth is sometimes dark and lonely and repulsive and desperate.

Last night I really didn't want to go to church. I was confused. *Why am I doing this again?* I asked myself. *I'm going for my husband. I'm going for my kids. I'm going because I love them, and they want to be there. It doesn't hurt me to be there, does it? How am I back in this questioning place again? I thought I had this church thing figured out.*

Tony and I dropped off our kids at their respective classes, and then we made our way to the front of the church to sit with some people we know. I noticed one of my good friends sitting in the very front next to her husband, who also happens to be a pastor at the church. I went up to talk to her before the service started. I asked her how she was doing, and she shared a little bit about the good stuff happening in her life right now. Then she asked me, placing her hand affectionately on my leg, "How are you?"

"I'm good," I said. But the words echoed through the internal chambers of my body, and they sounded back to me as, "That's a lie. That's a lie. That's a lie."

"Actually," I said to her, "I'm not good. I don't know why I said that. Today has been a very dark day. I feel very—"

I was interrupted as someone approached her to talk. I could tell it wasn't going to be a short conversation, so I put my hand on her shoulder and said, "It's really good to see you."

She looked at me apologetically and said, "We'll talk more soon."

She texted me later, after church, asking if I was doing okay. I was relieved I had told her the truth.

During the church service, I really struggled to pay attention. It was as though I was hearing everything with earmuffs on, muffled sounds with only half the message getting through. *I need help,* I thought, and my artist friend Valerie came to mind. I had been to visit Valerie once in her home in Northern California. We worked together as partners in an online company for a few years and got to know each other quite well through online tools like Instant Messenger and Skype. I dimmed my iPhone screen so as not to disrupt those around me in church, and I sent her a message through Facebook, letting her know I felt dark and alone and that I loved her and just wanted to know she was there.

To my surprise, she responded back immediately.

"I'd make you a peanut-butter sandwich," she said, which is what she had done for me in California a few years ago. She had packed me a lunch to eat in the airport as I waited for my plane to return home. Best peanut-butter-and-jelly sandwich I've ever had. Her Facebook message made me smile. Then another one came through.

"I am sorry you are feeling alone and dark. Skype me. I'm here."

"I'm at church. ;)," I told her, knowing she would find that ironic. How can I feel dark and alone when I'm in church?

"HA!" she responded. And then, "I think Jesus said that: 'Skype Me. I am here.'"

I smiled. *She's right, You know. Jesus, You are right here with me, and I'm feeling Your love through my California friend who is miles away from me. I'm feeling Your love through my friend who has a room in her home that she calls the Jesus room.*

I was thankful that Valerie, who on spiritual matters goes by the self-proclaimed title "Woo-Woo," was available last night to remind me that despite my darkness, I'm in close proximity to the Divine. Jesus is a Skype call away. We are never alone.

As I began writing this book, I blogged openly about my need to get some space away from other people so that I could hear my own voice and God therein. I alluded to the fact that there were some dark roads ahead of me and suggested that people might check on me from time to time to see if I was doing okay. This is the blog post that Tony's coworkers referred to when they called us in for a meeting.

When I initially wrote that blog post, several friends expressed their concern for me. A few of them even suggested we meet together for coffee so they could hear how I was doing. Even though I requested people to check in on me, my initial response to these meeting requests was to snap my shoulders back, stick my chin out, and push the red button to send my walls of defense flying up around me on all four sides. *What do you mean, am I okay? I'm finding out more about myself than I've ever known before. I'm actually taking care of my heart and listening to it. Of course I'm okay.*

I got a little scared. *Are they going to come fix me? Are they going to tell me my messy truth is out of line?*

Luckily, a softer, declawed version of myself reminded me, *You have nothing to hide. You are okay. You are not out of line or being deceitful or hypocritical. You are doing what you need to do to be true to yourself. You are seeking healing. You are seeking understanding. You are seeking God and listening to what you believe is His voice to the best of your ability. You are loving where He has you. Why would you not tell them the truth? What are you so ashamed of?*

I was able to relax. I was able to be okay with my truth—a truth that didn't match up to the truth I had memorized about what a good Christian's life should look like.

I know it doesn't make sense that I should be doing okay when I've taken away many of the pillars of Christianity, but I really am doing okay. Even better than okay. Even in the dark moments, like last night, when I was depressed and felt a little crazy, as if I might just run away from everything I once held dear, I still know this is where I want to be, and I really and truly trust God with me here. It's a shaky sort of trust, but it's all I've got.

Chapter Nineteen

Friend

At the outset of this awakening journey, which I believe really took off in October of 2010, I also made a good friend. I've mentioned Teresa off and on throughout this book because she has been an integral part of my journey. Our friendship actually began online. After my Angry Homemade Noodles episode in 2008, I started a six-week online study for moms via my blog. Using my own anger and brokenness after my fourth child as a catalyst for discussion and community, I entered into a very healing and eye-opening time in my life as a woman. I began to see women as comrades instead of competition.

I have certainly had friendships with women throughout the entirety of my marriage, but they were always secondary to my relationship with my husband. I had this assumption that to honor my marriage, I must see Tony as supreme confidant. I had this bias that women were catty creatures who would rip you apart in an instant if given the opportunity. They weren't to be trusted. They were cliquish, superficial, and dramatic. They were flaky, weak, and moody. They were often clueless and selfish and made foolish deci-sions based on emotional responses. They had issues I couldn't relate to, because I was strong, independent, and one with my husband, who was entirely masculine and had his own eye-roll moments at the messiness of women.

Of course, all of these assumptions weren't really verbalized. They were buried deep, too deep to put a name to them. Too deep to recognize their effects on my own choices. I believe the assumptions were formed long before marriage even. They were formed when I was a young teen and so badly wanted to be liked by boys and found my connection to them in scrappy neighborhood games of pickup basketball, where I was sometimes the only girl playing. They were formed through religious reminders that men were the ones who assumed the leadership roles, and Eve was the one who made the first sinful mistake. They were formed through silly, little junior high spats that felt neither silly nor little at the time and made me wonder if there were such a thing as a girlfriend who could be trusted. They were formed by reminders that good girls don't draw attention to themselves. They were formed by other immeasurable conversations and observations.

I continued through life with several strong women acquain-tances, the majority of them Christian women. I would indeed call them friends, and many of them I am still in communication with, but the lines of friendship only went as deep as I would let them. It's impossible to make a close lady friend if subconsciously you believe she only wants to chew you up and spit you out. But more important, it's impossible to make a close lady friend if you believe you don't deserve one, don't desire one, and couldn't possibly be one yourself. I had this strange inclination that any admission of needing a girlfriend would be an outright betrayal to my marriage. I was afraid of the fact that women were different from men and scared to admit I was included in those differences. I was scared, and yet I was lonely in ways I couldn't put a finger on.

The Angry Homemade Noodles group began as a cry for help on my blog. I wondered if I was dealing with postpartum depression. I truly think it was the first time I felt like I needed the understanding of other women. *Am I going crazy? Please, someone tell me I'm not going crazy.* I braced myself for the "Pull yourself together" advice I thought I might receive. The Christian answer I expected was "Don't fall apart, because your husband needs you to be the keeper of the home, and being the keeper means you'll hold it all together." It was, of course, the answer I had been giving myself for years. Weak women fall apart. Strong women hold it together. I wanted kids, didn't I? I wanted lots of them, so this is the web I had woven for myself. *Face it, sister. You got what you asked for; you best be able to handle it.*

But in my broken moment, where answers failed me, I wondered if I was just another victim of the plastic-coated, perfectionistic promises of our world. I wondered if there were any other women who felt called to something larger than themselves and yet felt too broken to live any of it out. I needed a safe place to start asking questions, to start digging back the dirt, to start wondering, *Why, oh why, can I not love myself?* And my blogging community became that place. These were women who knew me. It didn't matter that I had just moved to a new state, because I had a web of womanly acquaintances online, and so I went to that web.

I was shocked and touched by their responses. My open admission of a vicious anger toward my children and an unhappiness with the life I was living didn't elicit disappointment or disgust or disapproval. In fact, something amazing happened. Other women began to share their own similar situations and were relieved I had given them a platform to admit and discuss them. I wasn't met by foolish, catty, weak women; I was met by other women who were telling me I was strong to reach out, strong to admit my mood swings, and strong to believe there was something better for me. The healing instantly began in my life the day I wrote that haunting blog post admitting my defeat, and it was the catalyst to a renewed effort to love these mysterious creatures called females, including myself.

Teresa was a part of the original Angry Homemade Noodles. She found me through my blog and, though in a different season of mothering altogether with her children all grown, she was attracted to the invitation to forgive herself for imperfect moments she'd had with her own children. There was to be much more to our relationship, but the orchestration of that was going on beneath the surface, completely unbeknownst to us.

The Angry Homemade Noodles group morphed into many different shapes after the six-week study ended, and it continued in one form or another for a year, at which point I became tired of it. I admitted this to the group, fighting off the performance voices telling me these ladies needed this, and I would fall apart if I didn't have it, and I'd be a failure if I ended it. I ended it anyway. I had to. I wasn't feeling it anymore. Unknowingly, God was sending me into new seasons that would require every ounce of my extra time.

Seasons of honing myself as an artist. Seasons of reading and learning intimately about grace. And of course, this season of sifting through who I am and what my faith in God even means. I remember so vividly receiving a Google Talk message from Teresa, telling me what a brave thing I had done by ending the group. I tried not to read too much into it. Like, was she saying she never liked it to begin with? Was she saying it wasn't living up to anyone's expectations? I decided to instead take it as the compliment it was intended to be, the confirmation that it was, in fact, time to move on.

Not too long after that, Teresa contacted me privately, saying she'd love to extend our friendship, and would I be interested in a mentoring sort of relationship. We actually live in close proximity, so the possibility of meeting in person was even an option, but I've already explained to you my issues with women. And though the healing had begun in my heart, I couldn't see mentorship as anything different from what it had been to me previously: a way to hold me accountable to all the rules I wasn't sure I believed in anymore. A way to make sure I was staying in my place. A way to be coached by a woman who was ahead of me in life and, therefore, had all the answers.

While I was beginning to believe I did need a few close women to journey through life with, I was beginning to doubt whether those women needed to be Christian. I wasn't about to get myself caught up in another legalistic chain of have-tos and good wifely, motherly devotion, so over a course of a couple of emails back and forth, where she assured me she didn't think this was supposed to look like any sort of mentorship she or I had ever been a part of, I ended up declining. I can't even remember if I let her know I was declining. I might have just not responded. Or perhaps I should say, my response was just delayed. Nine months delayed!

In October I felt I was ready for a confidante and instantly thought of Teresa. I humbly asked if the offer still stood and waded in gently as she graciously did the same. We met in person for the first time one night over chocolate cupcakes. For years I didn't care much for chocolate. I think it was a subconscious rebellious choice, because chocolate was something women were gaga over, and I wasn't about to admit I was a member of that sordid, weak sex. But let me tell you, that first night with Teresa, chocolate never tasted so good.

I went into our relationship with many inhibitions. My expectations were low, and my walls were high. I didn't need or want to be fixed. I didn't want help. I didn't think I even wanted to be loved. I just wanted someone to talk to who would "get" my artist heart and confirm me in continuing in the direction I felt God was calling me.

Teresa was gentle and graceful. She didn't attempt to rein me in. I remember the time I emailed her and told her I thought I was a rebel, and that God was okay with that, and I asked her what she thought about it. I'm not sure I was seeking her approval as much as I was testing whether she would lecture me or confirm me. I knew there were truths about myself I had to dive into and face, and I wanted to know if she was a safe person to go there with. Would she run? Would she try to fix me? Would she shake her head in disappointment? She did none of those things.

Just nine months after our rebellious conversation, our relationship is at an entirely different level. She has walked through this book-writing process with me, this spiritual awakening. She has seen many of the darks and the lights of me. She has watched me wrestle with God and with myself. She has allowed my anger to fume, sometimes even at her, and has refused to judge me for it. Last night I sent her a few lines from a poem I found. It speaks to the level our friendship has reached, something I never could have anticipated:

> The rebel in you
> energizes
> the rebel in me.
>
> That long-removed
> satisfied, carefree
> sleeping rebel of mine.
> I feel it stirring.
>
> Yes—
> that gut-wrenching music
> of your rebel
> has invaded me
> shaken and reminded me
> there are other ways
> to live.[1]

When I met Teresa, I thought she was the perfect Christian woman with her *T*s all crossed, her *I*s all dotted, her rules all followed, and her lessons all learned. The person I have come to know is a woman who dances bravely in the face of vulnerability and anger and pain. She has given me the greatest gift a friend can give—her raw true self—and it has allowed me to be my raw true self. The way I understand it, the term *namaste* is used to communicate a bowing to another's true self in deep respect and unity. The true self is the self uninhibited by ego or expectation. Namaste acknowledges that glorious potential in a human to give up one's ego and settle into a grace and freedom that unites us all. Teresa is this namaste friend to me.

By choosing to remain my friend now, after all we've been through, it's as if she is saying to me, "I know you can be more than your imperfections, your hurts, your bad habits, your inconsistencies. I recognize you already as a person stepping into your fullest potential. As an artwork created by God. As a vessel filled with Christ. As a person who is whole." And I am saying the same thing back to Teresa as we seek to collaborate with each other.

Namaste is a statement of humility, because in saying it, I am admitting I'm not better than another. It's also a statement of confidence, because in saying it, I am stating that another has something valuable to offer the world. It's a hopeful statement. It's a prayer. It is, for me, a belief that God created us and is constantly making us new, and it's the choice to see each other in that light.

My namaste friendship did not develop overnight. It did not develop by force. It certainly did not develop because of anything I arranged. There is no formula for creating friendships such as these, but I do wonder if they appear only when we're ready for them. I had gotten to a place in my own life where I knew what God was telling me, even if it scared the hell out of me, and I knew I was in a very fragile state. Being around anyone who would crush my dreams or discount the words I was hearing from God would have been detrimental to my health.

I had come to a personal confidence I had never known before. A confidence that God does indeed speak to me and does indeed want to use me in the midst of my mess. I needed someone who wouldn't walk in with mop and broom and start to clean me up, but who would encourage and even dare me to walk down narrow, slanted sidewalks of broken concrete and weedy crevices. I couldn't have put all that into words before meeting Teresa, but in hindsight, I realize this is what she has done for me. She has acted as a sort of birth coach, a midwife who has coaxed life to the full (and consequently this book) out of me. I believe God knew that this sidewalk was going to intimidate me at times, especially because so many others seem to be walking down the freshly laid, perfect sidewalks. I believe He knew I would need a friend to travel with me. He knew before I knew that it *always* helps to have a friend repeating for you the truths you want to believe for yourself.

I believe God also knew that I needed a lady friend. There were feminine wounds in me that needed to be healed. Wounds I had no idea existed. I was reading the book *The Dance of the Dissident Daughter* by Sue Monk Kidd[2] when I first started to clue in to this feminine piece of my awakening puzzle. I realized I had always felt like the lesser sex, despite my father's repeated encouragement to me as a child that I would be the first woman president. I didn't believe it for myself, and he couldn't instill confidence in me. I felt I was just a shadow dweller. An underling for the real carriers of wisdom—men. Sue put words to feelings that had gone unnoticed by me for years. She clued in to my misunderstandings of who God is.

I can remember texting Teresa one day, asking her if she was a feminist, asking her if she thought God was. The idea of God having a feminine side was amazingly comforting. I was moved by the idea that my emotional responses, my allurement to mystery and romance, and my desires to nurture and cultivate growth were valid and needed and a part of God's character. I was intrigued by a feminine side of God because I so badly needed someone to show me how to be what author and artist Sark would call "a succulent, wild woman."[3]

I had avoided looking face-to-face at my own feminimity for far too long. I needed to not be afraid of it, disappointed by it, or embarrassed that it might leak out onto others and taint them in some way. I was relieved that it might be considered natural and lovely and necessary to embrace being a woman and all the depths of self-discovery that would entail. In many ways, Teresa became God with skin on for me, and as I eased into her love for me, I simultaneously eased into God's feminine love for me. Women weren't the enemy. They also weren't the only solution. They were a part of the whole. A part I had been missing.

Another thing Teresa did for me was to ensure my sanity. When you choose to enter into the dark places searching for your own soul, and when you decide you must walk on cracked, crooked sidewalks, and when you claim to hear God's voice perhaps not audibly but definitely clearly, you need someone to reassure you that you have not gone off the deep end. Teresa encourages me to dance even though others may not be able to feel the rhythm I do. It's my own unforced rhythm directed by what I believe to be an extraordinary mixture of my spirit and the Divine's Spirit swirling inside me.

I have even found it a relief to know that at times my own husband won't hear the music I am hearing. This too doesn't make me crazy. We are different breeds, man and woman, and that is okay. Finally I believe that it's okay. It is so nice to have a lady friend to understand the parts of me that Tony just can't possibly get. I no longer feel threatened or discounted by those parts of me he can't understand. I also no longer feel the need to defend, convince, or be listened to by Tony ad nauseam. I don't need his validation on every premonition, intuition, or revelation. He seems to prefer hearing way fewer words, and I'm now able to give him way fewer words. He can still know me as his wife, but I am able to give him the summaries instead of the sorting.

This realization occurred to me one night when Tony and I were on a coffee date at Starbucks. Two young adult women sat to the left of us, chatting about everything under the sun but largely about selling makeup. As we were leaving the coffee shop, Tony laughed and said, "I don't think those two girls ever took a breath."

To which I replied, smiling mysteriously, "That's exactly what Teresa and I sound like when we're together."

My times with Teresa are magical, and I try not to use that word lightly. Something transpires between us; a third sort of being or wisdom or muse seems to emerge as we do life in tandem. Random texts, emails, photos, phone calls, and person-to-person encounters are all generated by this unforced rhythm of God's grace. What I mean by that is we don't seem to have rules to our friendship, or deadlines or time lines or procedures. Things happen as they happen, and they always seem to happen right as they need to. Each of us unfolding in our own lives, taking daring steps of bravery and vulnerability and artistry, and consequently, each of us unfolding into each other's lives. There is plenty of space and yet plenty of closeness.

This isn't unlike the friendship I have with my husband, and I'm amazed that it is possible to have this friendship with a woman as well. I am blessed by the treasures I am given every time I interact with Teresa.

It feels delicious to have a lady friend who comes alongside me as I learn how to settle in and be myself, my true self. She certainly epitomizes every bit of the phrase *anam cara*, which means *soul friend* in Gaelic. I would be lying, though, if I told you we never have our moments of doubt. There are times when we both have admitted to wondering how vulnerable we want to be, for fear the other person will turn and run, leaving us naked and ashamed.

Teresa and I got together just this past weekend. It had been a couple of weeks since we had last seen each other. We'd tried to get together twice, but Teresa had been unable to meet, once due to an unfortunate MS flare-up, and once due to another commitment she needed to honor with her son. I was surprised how vulnerable and nervous I felt as I approached the restaurant door. I grabbed the handle and peered through the window. I saw Teresa seated inside. She smiled and waved at me, and my heart flooded with emotion. Did I dare tell her how nervous I'd been? Did I dare confess to her how terrified I was that she no longer needed my friendship? Did I dare admit how many conversations I'd had with God to convince myself I could do life without her if I had to?

I took a deep breath and opened the door. As I approached the table, she said to me, "Okay, this can never happen again. I know we're antirules and all, but we have to make a rule that we can't go this long without meeting ever again. This was brutal."

I threw myself down beside her on the bench like an overdramatic actress, tossed the back of my hand up to my forehead, and said, "Okay, I wasn't going to tell you this, but I was totally freaking out. I thought you were over me."

She giggled. "Oh, Lord, have we become codependent?" she asked, rolling her eyes.

"Oh, gosh, I hope not. Please don't tell me we are codependent. I mean, I could do life without you, I just really don't want to," I said.

I had a friend tell me recently that the difference between collaboration and codependency is that in collaboration both people are leaning into each other with equal vulnerability. Both people are risking. In codependency, it's really just one person leaning. I think Teresa and I are both leaning in deep, and that's what makes this so scary and so fulfilling.

Teresa and I both have histories of friendships gone sour that we can refer to and pull from and wonder, *Will this new friendship turn out the same?* It's part of the risk, I suppose, and so far the calculated costs of that risk haven't been enough to scare either of us away. In fact, sometimes I think they have made us lean in all the more, hunkering down like two children under a homemade blanket fort, turning on our flashlights when either of us gets scared, and pointing them at each other as if to say, "I'm still here. Are you still here?" We are both still here, and interestingly enough, the fort seems to be expanding, and we find ourselves reaching outward and extending some blanket to others who may have never known a secret club such as this.

I remember, as a grade-school child, being warned against making a "best friend," because then you are limiting yourself to one friendship, and it could be very lonely if and when the best friend should ever leave you. I hear this little warning every now and then, and I wonder if it still applies—or if it ever did. What I know to be true today is that this relationship is breathing life and breadth into my persona and expanding my ability to love and include others, not limiting it. So for now I must ignore the warnings of my youth and press into what I'm being given, a precious gift of friendship with another woman. A lady friend who is teaching me how to be loved and accepted, not only by her, but also by myself, by the feminine nature of God, by my husband, and by countless others. I believe in many ways it is much harder to learn to be loved than it is to learn to love. The first always precedes the second.

Chapter Twenty

Self-Portraits

I recently met with a friend of mine for coffee. We are still relatively new friends, wading through the awkward getting-to-know-you phase as best we can with our limited time away from our families and other responsibilities. Besides our family roles as wives and mothers, we have art in common, and it is this love of art that has sort of woven our lives together. My friend is a talented portrait artist. Her house is full of lovely framed paintings and drawings she has created. But I'm getting to know her at an interesting time in her life. She has hit a sort of lull, as all of us artists do from time to time, and she is searching for the inspiration and motivation to get out her paints and continue once again. She is asking questions like "Why do I paint? Who am I doing this for? What is the purpose? What do I want to do with my art? Where do I begin again?"

As we met that night, a thought occurred to me, so I shared it with her. "Maybe you begin with yourself," I told her. "Start painting self-portraits." She smiled politely. I could tell the gears were turning in her head, mulling over my suggestion. "It's just an idea," I said, "but I have this image of you painting portrait after portrait after portrait of yourself. So many that you have these giant stacks of thick artist paper lying around your studio."

She mentioned earlier that sometimes she would paint and give the paintings away as Christmas presents. We joked that this year everyone would be receiving portraits of her for their gifts. "You can just explain to them that you were doing a self-study."

I realized as I was talking to her that the idea sounded exactly like what I need. I'd had a rough day being a mom and struggling to figure out how to model my faith for my kids when I don't even know what I believe anymore. I'd almost canceled the coffee-shop date with my friend altogether but decided the last thing I needed was to stay in the house with my kids even longer, trying to force some miracle of clarity to occur. I opted to go for coffee, but only if I let myself go in my most comfortable attire of hooded sweatshirt, jeans, and tennis shoes. My hair was in a sloppy ponytail, my makeup rather forlorn. I decided if we were to be friends, she'd just as well see me at my worst as at my best. Sitting in the chilly coffee shop listening to my new and beautiful friend talk about her own self-identity confusion, I started to get some answers for myself. Good friends are able to do that—open your eyes to things you needed to see but couldn't manage on your own.

In the weeks to come, I thought more about the self-portrait idea. I realized I may have been suggesting it to her because it was something I so desperately needed for myself. The problem was when I thought about doing it for myself, it felt a little vain, conceited, self-indulgent. Do I really need to focus on me even more? Haven't I had enough of that? The thought even occurred to me, *I've returned to church, so I must be fixed now. I'm out of the dark place. I've moved on, right?* I laughed at my own analysis. Just because I've returned to church doesn't mean I love it or understand it or understand myself while I'm there. It's far more messy than that. I'm in church because I want to be there to honor my husband and what he is committed to at this time in our lives. I ask God every week, "Am I going back again?" As long as He says yes, I'll return. But just because I believe I'm hearing God's voice and obeying it doesn't mean I'm fixed. Things still feel so messy.

This past weekend I had an interesting conversation with Teresa. "Why am I back in a dark place again?" I asked her, somewhat annoyed that I was even having this conversation. I'm writing a whole book about being in a dark place, and I thought the point was to work my way out of this dark place and move on with my life. Now I feel like I'm getting ready to write the final chapter, and I feel just as lost and moody as when I started. With exasperation in my voice, I asked, "Did I write it all for nothing?"

She looked at me, her eyes caring and understanding, the edges of her lips turned up in a gentle smile. Oh, I knew that look. I had seen it often over the past months. It was the look I have both come to love and hate. It is my ego that hates it. The look means I still have more to learn. It means I have not arrived. It means someone knows me well enough to see that I don't have it all figured out, put together, smoothed to a shine. My ego wants to wage war with that look.

Oh, you think you know me, do you? Oh, you think you're wiser than I am just because you've lived longer? Oh, you think you can tell me what to do?

She's a vicious thing, my ego, with claws that emerge with valor to defend the me that she assumes is under attack. Of course, the childlike free spirit inside of me loves the look. The look means I am going to be gathered up and held for a bit, allowed to take a break, allowed to rest my own weary feet that have been taking tiny steps up a giant hill. The free spirit doesn't get offended; she just twirls and takes naps and accepts things as they are. I tried to concentrate on that side of me as Teresa began to talk.

"What are you wanting, Mandy? What are you expecting out of all of this? To be perfect? To achieve Martha Stewart status where you've cleaned everything up and put everything in its place, and everything actually stays there, all neat and tidy and beautiful? Tell me, what are you expecting?"

My ego thought she was asking viciously, attacking me with her words. My ego thought her smile was sarcastic, and that her head was tilted as if to say, "I know it all." I didn't want to listen to my ego, though, because I wanted to really get this. I wanted to really understand this part. I wanted to know why I was in a dark place again, and if this was to be expected, how I could possibly come to terms with it and make my peace once and for all. I have a feeling there is no "once and for all," though, ever, and maybe that is what I need to realize.

"You're still trying to do this on your own," she mentions to me later in our conversation.

"Really? Am I? Still?" I'm disappointed with myself. Why won't I just let others help me?

"Yes, still," she says quietly, smiling. In these moments, she is the Sean Maguire to my good Will Hunting. She is the therapy I don't want and can't possibly need. She is the hug when I don't want to be hugged. The gentle words of "It's not your fault" repeated over and over and over again, boldly ignoring my replies of "I know, I know, I know."[1] She continues to repeat the same things to me over and over and over again. It is the repetition; it is the cyclical motion; it is the twisting staircase she descends to get inside my heart. And she doesn't stop, because she inherently knows I don't want her to, though my ego is doing its best to build walls and barricades and strongholds. She repeats it, and each time I utter the words, "I know," the words become a little weaker than my last, until at some point, I realize I don't know. I really don't know. I don't know how to let others love me. I don't know how to love myself. I don't know that I am enough, today, right in this present moment. I don't know that I am okay, especially after writing an entire book about figuring out how to be okay and then coming to the end of it to find out I haven't solved a thing. And she tells me again, "It's not your fault. You haven't failed. You are loved. This is life. This is messy life."

I heard that trigger word *messy*, and I lashed out for a minute. "Oh no. Messy is not my life. *Messy* is a word I picked to focus on for one year—2011. One year of mess, and then I can move on." My words sounded hollow upon the completion of my sentence. Did I really think I was going to clean this all up? I really did think I would. I realized I had myself cornered. I have written myself into a memoir of imperfect proportions, and it is just as quickly playing out before me in real life. Let me out. Someone wake me from this nightmare. If the mess continues to build, I might just break.

I become cognizant that I *am* still doing this on my own. I'm not surrendering; I am biding my time, counting the days until the year ends, and I can return on my merry little way. As I type this, I look to my left at my husband's desk. It is piled with papers and cycling paraphernalia and books and plastic bags and hangers and pens and technology gadgets. I haven't touched it for months. It's the living testimony of a busy life. It is also the living testimony of my allowing things to get messy. I haven't rushed to clean it or sort it or fix it. I have let it be. I thought I was letting it be because I was okay with things being messy now, but this is only a half-truth. I am okay with things being messy now as long as they are going to be cleaned up when this year ends, and we can all get back to life as it should be. I'm okay for a period of time that has been preapproved by my hypercontrolling homemaker meter, but I'm lying to myself if I say a day hasn't gone by when I haven't thought about cleaning up the mess. How long can I breathe through this, and am I really even breathing at all or just holding my breath?

The release hits me now. There is often a release after my ego has worked itself up into a frenzied ball of strained muscles and angry eyebrows. I can't do this. I can't write books with answers. I can't live life without messes. I can't waltz through without friends. I can't keep expecting these impossible things from myself. I'm tired again. I'm burned-out all over again. I'm never satisfied with enough. Enough is never enough. I am never enough in the present tense. Grace is always some elusive thing I'm running after. Why can't it be here with me now? Why can't I stop thrashing about with God when things get dark and life throws far more questions than answers at me, and all I have the energy to do is stare at blank walls and wonder why I'm not playing with my kids or doing yoga or cooking our supper? Why can't I love me in the moments when I simply need to rest?

Why can't I love me in the midst of my mistakes? Why am I only lovely in the moments when I'm doing life as it's meant to be done?

I return to my idea of self-portraits. I want my own stacks of self-portraits to study, but I am still leery. I realize the truth behind my leeriness. It isn't that I am arrogant or self-absorbed or conceited. These are the excuses I use for why I cannot "go there," when in reality I cannot "go there" because it would mean looking at myself far too closely. Staring at myself naked in a mirror, much like I began this whole journey. It would mean I would have to take in flaws, but more important, it would also mean I would have to take in beauty. I haven't let myself find beauty there. I have been so fixated on working through my mess so I could move on that I have forgotten to love me right in the midst of the mess. I want to study myself. I want to find the things that are there to love even on the gray days that return when I thought I had moved past them. Especially on these gray days.

Perhaps I should photograph myself every time I feel defeated. Perhaps I should photograph myself every time I feel like a failure. Perhaps I should sketch myself on the days when I've slipped into my "Beware of God" T-shirt and my eyeliner is smudged from crying. Perhaps I should photograph myself every time the mess feels like it has returned, and the darkness threatens that this time it will in fact swallow me, because if it is back again, then surely it has won.

Instead of letting the darkness remind me of my apparent inability to overcome, I will take a picture and find a reason to love even now, especially now. Maybe if I make a concerted effort to meet myself eye to eye and say, "I love you," then I can believe it. Then I can leave myself alone. Then I can breathe through the mess instead of holding my breath until it passes, all the while wondering what I could have done to avoid it in the first place.

Or maybe … maybe this is just me saying, "I know, I know, I know," when in fact I don't know, and I can't possibly know until I am here again, and I'm hearing a friend or the Divine or my husband whisper in my ear, "It's not your fault." I don't think I can love myself by myself. As much as I want to do this on my own, I will never outgrow the need to be reminded "It's not your fault" and "You are lovely despite the mess." I need others' cyclical reminders to wash filters of love over my tainted self-portraits so that I may once again find my peace amidst a messy memoir written in blood and smeared with tears of both sorrow and joy. Like Henry Miller said, "The world would only begin to get something of value from me the moment I stopped being a serious member of society and became—myself."[2]

"There are things to love here, even here," I say under my breath, staring at my blank walls, smothered in seas of gray. "Even in the mess, I am enough." And realizing this … why, I do believe this is what it means to skip dangerously down that narrow path and to live fully alive. I'm invigorated by the dark places. I want to feel everything. The mysterious ebbs and flows. The games of freeze tag in frozen parks and the click-clacking of alleged prostitute heels. The feminine and the masculine. "The true and the questions,"as Sabrina Ward Harrison would suggest.[3] The darks and the lights. This is not a game of fix it and forget it; this is an embracing of it all, an acceptance of every rebellious inclination the Divine stirs up within me. This is permission to settle into my one messy life and make something of it.

Notes

Chapter One: Dear Friend

1. Joni Mitchell, "Both Sides Now," *Clouds* (New York: Siquomb, 1969).
2. C. S. Lewis, *The Horse and His Boy* (New York: Collier Books, 1970), 158–59.

Chapter Two: Full

1. Anne Lamott, *Plan B: Further Thoughts on Faith* (New York: Penguin, 2005), 20.
2. Joan Osborne, "One of Us," *Relish* (Island / Mercury, 1995).

Chapter Three: You

1. Rick Warren, *The Purpose Driven Life* (Grand Rapids: Zondervan, 2002), 17.
2. Jon Heder, in *Napoleon Dynamite*, directed by Jared Hess (Los Angeles: Fox Searchlight Pictures and Paramount, 2004), DVD.
3. Frederick Buechner, *Telling the Truth: The Gospel as Tragedy, Comedy, and Fairy Tale* (New York: HarperOne, 1977), 7.

Chapter Five: Voice

1. William P. Young, *The Shack* (Newbury Park, CA: Windblown Media, 2007), 195.

Chapter Six: Running

1. Christian Slater and Mary Stuart Masterson, in *Bed of Roses*, directed by Michael Goldenberg (New York: New Line Cinema, 1996), DVD.

Chapter Seven: Illiterate

1. Brent Curtis and John Eldredge, *The Sacred Romance: Drawing Closer to the Heart of God* (Nashville: Thomas Nelson, 1997), 137–38.

Chapter Eight: Darkness

1. Chaim Potok, *My Name Is Asher Lev* (New York: Anchor Books, 2003), 17–18.

2. Potok, *Asher Lev*, chapter 4.

3. Potok, *Asher Lev*, 239.

4. Kate DiCamillo, *The Tale of Despereaux* (Cambridge, MA: Candlewick, 2003).

5. Madeleine L'Engle, *Walking on Water: Reflections on Faith and Art* (Wheaton, IL: Harold Shaw, 1980), 5.

6. Mary Oliver, "The Journey," in *Dream Work* (New York: Atlantic Monthly, 1986), 38.

7. Ian Gillan, "The Temple," in *Jesus Christ Superstar* (Original Studio Recording), composed by Andrew Lloyd Webber and Tim Rice (Santa Monica: Geffen, 1993).

8. Gregory Maguire, *Wicked: The Life and Times of the Wicked Witch of the West* (New York: HarperCollins, 1995), 357.

9. Robert Henri, *The Art Spirit* (New York: Basic Books, 1951), 44.

10. Idina Menzel, "Defying Gravity," in *Wicked* (Original Broadway Cast Recording), composed by Stephen Schwartz, (New York: Universal Classics Group, 2003).

Chapter Nine: Toast

1. Rainer Maria Rilke, *Letters to a Young Poet* (New York: W. W. Norton, 1954), 27.

2. Madeleine L'Engle, *A Wrinkle in Time* (New York: Farrar, Straus, and Giroux, 1962).

Chapter Ten: So?

1. Gerald G. May, *Addiction and Grace: Love and Spirituality in the Healing of Addictions* (New York: HarperOne, 1988), 14–15

Chapter Eleven: Mystery

1. John O'Donohue, "The Inner Landscape of Beauty," interview by Krista Tippett, *On Being*, January 26, 2012, http://www.onbeing.org/program/inner-landscape-beauty/203.

2. William P. Young, *The Shack* (Newbury Park, CA: Windblown Media, 2007), 203.

3. Mary Shelley, *Frankenstein* (New York: Bantam, 2003), 7.

4. Young, *The Shack*, 182.

5. Gerald G. May, *Addiction and Grace: Love and Spirituality in the Healing of Addictions* (New York: HarperOne, 1988), 31.

6. Walt Whitman, "O Me! O Life!," *Complete Poems of Walt Whitman* (Hertfordshire, UK: Wordsworth Editions, 1995), 205.

Chapter Twelve: Love

1. Meister Eckhart, *Meister Eckhart: A Modern Translation*, trans. Raymond B. Blakney (New York: Harper & Row, 1941), 10.

2. Keri Smith, *Mess: The Manual of Accidents and Mistakes* (New York: Perigee, 2010).

Chapter Thirteen: Childlike

1. *Ratatouille*, directed by Brad Bird and Jan Pinkava (Pixar Animation Studios / Walt Disney Pictures, 2007).

Chapter Fourteen: Belong

1. John O'Donohue, *Anam Cara* (New York: HarperCollins, 1997), 36.

2. O'Donohue, *Anam Cara*, 47.

3. O'Donohue, *Anam Cara*, 34.

4. William P. Young, *The Shack* (Newbury Park, CA: Windblown Media, 2007), 181.

5. *Mona Lisa Smile*, directed by Mike Newell (Revolution Studios / Columbia Pictures, 2003).

6. Antoine de Saint-Exupéry, *The Little Prince*, trans. Richard Howard (Hertfordshire, England: Wordsworth Editions, 1995).

Chapter Fifteen: Labeled

1. St. John of the Cross, *Dark Night of the Soul*, trans. E. Allison Peers (New York: DoubleDay, 2005), 192.

2. Julie Andrews, in *Mary Poppins*, directed by Robert Stevenson (Walt Disney, 1964).

3. Madeleine L'Engle, *Walking on Water: Reflections on Faith and Art* (Wheaton, IL: Harold Shaw, 1980),118.

4. L'Engle, *Walking on Water*, 117–18.

Chapter Sixteen: Rhythms

1. Anne Morrow Lindbergh, *Gift from the Sea* (New York: Pantheon Books, 2005), 100–101.

2. Teresa Robinson, *Right Brain Planner*, www.rightbrainplanner.com.

3. John O'Donohue, *Anam Cara* (New York: HarperCollins, 1997), 84–85.

4. Shaun Tan, *The Red Tree* (Australia: Lothian, 2010).

Chapter Seventeen: Conversations

1. Joaquin Phoenix and Mel Gibson, in *Signs*, directed by M. Night Shyamalan (Buena Vista Pictures, 2002).

2. Mandy Steward, "I'm Tired of Being a Christian," *Messy Canvas* (blog), December 3, 2010, http://www.messycanvas.com/2010/12/im-tired-of-being-a-christian/.

3. Robert Frost, "Mending Wall," *The Poetry of Robert Frost: The Collected Poems, Complete and Unabridged* (New York: Henry Holt, 1969), 33.

4. Elizabeth Gilbert, *Eat, Pray, Love: One Woman's Search for Everything Across Italy, India and Indonesia* (New York: Penguin, 2006), 208.

5. Gilbert, *Eat, Pray, Love*.

Chapter Eighteen: Truth

1. Natalie Goldberg, *Writing Down the Bones: Freeing the Writer Within* (Boston: Shambhala Publications, Inc., 1986), 40.

Chapter Nineteen: Friend

1. Sherrie Lovler, "Another Awakening," *Nature, Art, and Poetry* (blog), November 2, 2010, http://natureartandpoetry.blogspot.com/2010/11/another-awakening.html.

2. Sue Monk Kidd, *The Dance of the Dissident Daughter: A Woman's Journey from Christian Tradition to the Sacred Feminine* (New York: HarperCollins, 1996).

3. Sark, *Succulent Wild Woman: Dancing with Your Wonder-Full Self* (New York: Fireside, 1997).

Chapter Twenty: Self-Portaits

1. Robin Williams and Matt Damon, in *Good Will Hunting* (Miramax Films, 1997).

2. Henry Miller, *Sexus: The Rosy Crucifixion* (New York: Grove Press, 1965), 206.

3. Sabrina Ward Harrison, *The True and the Questions: A Journal* (San Francisco: Chronicle Books, 2005.)